"Against All Odds"

Becoming More Than Your Experiences

De'Vord J Allen

AGAINST ALL ODDS - Becoming More Than Your Experiences
De'Vord J Allen

© Copyright 2018 by Published by Chloe Arts and Publishing, LLC

Richfield MN. 55423

Library of Congress: 18234814401
ISBN: 978-09991829-8-7(Paperback)
Printed United States of America

Chloe Arts and Publishing, LLC
Write the vision make it plain. Habakkuk 2:2

AGAINST ALL ODDS

Chapter Index

*Contact Us: DeVordJAllen@gmail.com

DEDICATION

This book is dedicated to those who are the driving force of my life.

First, my God and Savior whom through Him all things become possible.

To my wonderful children who give me purpose daily/sometimes hourly when I am off track. I love you all the way past the sky!

To all my friends, extended families who believed in me through my darkest moments.

"Last but not least to the 'Dream Killers' for always giving me the determination to persevere." "Against all odds."

As I wrote this book, I searched my soul to find inspiration to speak from my heart. May these pages, touch someone and may a life be saved. Stay strong and keep God first. Hope you enjoy!

FOREWORD BY "MARK BLANKESPOOR"

I had the privilege of living in the same federal prison housing unit with DeVord Allen. Living 24/7 with guys, especially during the lockdown challenges of the COVID-19 pandemic, provided a window to their true character and personality. I have been greatly encouraged by DeVord's authenticity and consistency as we have become friends and have done life together. DeVord speaks from his heart and from the highs and lows of his personal experience. He does not project theory; he shares the reality of his tangible life events. He has experienced various storms in his life, but those storms have not overtaken him. The storms have been crucible experiences that provided him a clear focus of a life that includes great meaning and true significance.

My hope for you as your read DeVord's book is that regardless of your past mistakes or difficulties, you can appreciate the opportunity to step into a life of meaning and significance. Your life truly matters. DeVord will share valuable insights including:

1. We are all given chances in this life to do something with our future, regardless of the mistakes we have made in the past.
2. Our mistakes do not need to define us.
3. We can truly become the people we always dreamed of becoming regardless of where we may be.

DeVord helped me grasp more fully that my life mattered, even when I was in a deep, dark valley. I believe this book will encourage you to value how your life also matters. You are important. DeVord will affirm your significance. Enjoy the book and what you learn!

PREFACE

"Against All Odds" is an inspirational account of a man who would pay the ultimate expense for his illegal attempts to gain prosperity. This is his personal testimony of the transformational process he sought to gain redemption, evolving from the desolate "street life" of narcotics trafficking to a life of reverence and purpose. He shares vivid accounts of his life to teach us to become more than our experiences.

Allen shares the tools he uses daily for creating goals, challenging your thinking, and daily practices of establishing an open-minded approach to a win-win mindset, regardless of your current circumstances, "Against All Odds."

> *"Our mere existence is not coincidental; the essence of our being is to define and create that which brings purpose to our lives. Finding that purpose defines your journey"*
> ~DeVord J. Allen

INTRODUCTION

I n order to clearly understand where we are today, we must first assess the actions of yesterday. Accepting the choices we have made, opens the doors to ratification. You must begin where you are, and that journey starts with the first step.

The problems for me began at an early age. I was born an only child to a single, teenage mother. I think the term used when I was growing up was "latch key kid." Due to our economic state, I was left with the responsibility of getting to school on time, preparing my own meals at times, and making sure I finished my homework before bathing and going to bed. Most evenings, my mother would arrive home well after the hours I'd gone to bed. I would soon learn there were millions of other young men like myself spread throughout urban low-income neighborhoods and suburban section 8 housing areas alike, whom also, were raised by single, working mothers and had little to no structure in their lives other than sports or a family member to serve as a sitter.

As a result of problems associated with our financial circumstances, I was left with too much unsupervised leisure time. Though no fault of my mother, it's just economics. No father present or real 'role models' lead to misguided influences.

I was too young to fully comprehend the dynamics surrounding our community at that time. It was virtually impossible for me to conceive that my mother, like so many others, had inherited "generational poverty." Our continual struggle as a marginalized group would play a large part in my irrational behavior patterns. The realization of the culture that besieged us was simply "The haves and the have little to none."

Growing up I remember never wanting to attend school. I was ashamed of the clothing I was forced to wear simply because my mother had to shop at the "Goodwill." I remember the humiliation of eating free lunch at school and how we were separated in the lunch lines, one for kids whose parents could afford to buy lunch and the other line for the kids who were like me, eating the free lunch. Looking back on it all now makes little to no sense. I hated my life because we were poor. But, as I stated earlier, we are where we are in life today because of the choices and actions of yesterday.

My mind flashed back to the overcrowded elementary and middle school classrooms where I struggled to focus and often drifted, never seeming to grasp the lessons being taught. There'd be times when I'd get a restroom pass just to get out of class. To this day, I still don't know what all of that was about. But I do know it felt foreign to me. I wasn't a delayed learner or slower than the other classmates, I just lacked the excitement that most kids had with discovery learning. I think that there was, and still exists today, a lack of ability for non-ethnic educators to meet the needs and connect with diverse children, assisting in their individual learning styles. To some degree, real life lessons are missing from the curriculums. They often fail to teach so many of us from different cultures how choices and decisions will one day impact or dictate our futures. This, by no means, is an excuse or meant to blame others. I sincerely want to offer insightful information regarding the social-economic disparities and the burdens placed on the public school system in our urban communities. Because we sometimes use our emotions over intellect, we make unhealthy or wrong decisions. So many of our youth are faced with the same situations I've endured, growing up in poverty-stricken environments with minimal or no education and poor job skills. I, like so many others, chose the path of destruction that we dreamed of one day escaping.

While it is true that no one likes to struggle in life, we fail to envision adversity as a two-fold process. Some of our highest core values derive from the hardships we seek to escape. Such as the core value of "character" which defines who we are . . . during the obstacles. Or the core value of "integrity," correlates to being an . . . upstanding person of goodness remaining in uncompromised positioning. That is the first part of the process. The second part of the process is that hardship should be used to motivate and inspire, disallowing any excuse, more importantly, to serve and assist others who may also be underserved.

However, the process of struggle doesn't illustrate how many times we must go through a similar consequence to get to that point of growth. It becomes something we simply must go through. Like so many who had gone through the system before me, I'd use my past trauma as a crutch to justify and dictate my present and intended future.

It usually takes some type of tragedy to occur in order for someone who is doing wrong or not living right to step back, evaluate their lives, and think to do something to improve it.

CHAPTER ONE

How It All Began

My life really began to take a turn during junior high school. I became increasingly disengaged from my academics. I was never really more than a C student. My mind and focus always seemed to be anywhere but school.

I looked forward to attending school just to hang out with my friends. It all started with your typical misbehaving, skipping classes, and truancy. That led to suspensions and ensured my first interaction with the court system. I was placed on probation and received weekend work squad as punishment for the delinquent behaviors. Now, "work squad" is a program supervised by the courts. You're designated hours to work every Saturday in exchange for any fines or court-imposed penalties. You are required to report to your assigned work crew by 8:00 a.m. However, if you missed a Saturday or were asked to leave the assignment or detail, then the court would remand you into custody to serve your deferred sanction. Typically, you would be sent to the state's Juvenile Detention Center for a term of 90 days.

So, that was my introduction to the penal system. Most of the placements there were used as a deterrent from further villainous acts. But, for me it would become a continuous revolving cycle in and out of Juvenile Court, causing stress on my mother, and eventually leading the courts to remove me from my mother's care. I was sent to a children's shelter until the State found a foster care home for placement for me.

Now, here I was 12 years of age, locked in a room, surrounded by complete strangers, and expected to comply with the rules of the center. The first night in total isolation, I built a "mental fortress" which became my mode of survival. As an only child, I was accustomed to being alone. But I couldn't understand how the system could just take me away from my home and away from my mother. Once again, we couldn't help ourselves and there was no one to help us.

Eventually, they found placement for me. The first home was with a Caucasian family. I arrived late at night, and by morning I think the family had decided they didn't want to care for me. So, off I went back to the shelter to await another family for placement. Fortunately for me, I was placed in a nice home with a family of similar ethnic background. There were many children in this new home. But, from the initial intake the 'mother' of the house was very welcoming. She was a strong, single mother just like my own mother. However, it was clear that her vision and her goals were what separated her from my mother. My mother worked hard, but she worked for others. My foster mother owned multiple businesses and was highly respected amongst her colleagues within the foster care system. I would later discover how I was placed with her and her family. She was a widow who raised four children of her own and was a strict disciplinarian like my paternal mother. However, her punishments were never physical. She would rather require you to think through your actions and she would explain this was the reasoning behind the consequences. That whole experience was unknown to me. See, my mother believed if you did something wrong then you would be whipped with a belt or extension cord. This was her deterrent method, which never really seemed to work. To her defense, we adults tend to parent how we were parented unless we became educated to a different system of child rearing, allowing us to define our own beliefs concerning disciplining our children.

One of the many things I noticed living there was we all had chores and those chores would determine the allowance we each would receive on the first of every month. Unlike my mother, my foster mother never gave us money. You had to earn every dollar and if you failed at any assigned task, there would be no allowance. There were no exceptions to her rules. I also noticed we sat down and ate all meals together. There was a real sense of family structure that was absent in my home due to the fact my paternal mother would work until the late evening hours, leaving me to feed myself and be in bed before she got home from work. My foster mother was a very spiritual woman who would teach from the principles of her religious doctrine. She was present and believed in accountability. I learned so many invaluable lessons during my time there. Her entire family embraced me with love and support many years after I aged out of the foster care system.

At a certain age of emancipation, the Social Services Department gives an assessment to the court deeming the home fit for the child to return. So, my time had come for me to return home with my paternal mother. Nonetheless, I was experiencing a vexed amount of emotions. The fun I had at my mother's house on the weekends and the family structure . . . and presence I received in foster care, left me conflicted. Although I would often return and share time with my foster family, there was a real sense of disconnection for me at home now. It was almost as if there were two people inside of me: one social, the other solitary .

. . and reflective. At my mother's home, I loved hanging with my friends, going to parties, wearing nice clothes, and dating girls. The solitary side was drawn to my foster mother's home along with the teachings she shared, reading books, and working in her business to earn extra allowance.

Meanwhile, the façade of freedom and the defiant behaviors had once again taken a strong hold of me. I was now back at home with my mother and a freshman in high school. I was once again socializing with my old friends from the neighborhood, left without supervision or accountability.

I never intended to cause displeasure with either of my mother's; I had just become so vehement on doing things my own way.

I remember my first experience with weed and alcohol simultaneously. One weekend while my mother was working, I was hanging with my friend on a summer day. It was hot, we were bored. So another friend pulled out some weed and suggested we all get high. Although I sipped a few beers previously, I'd never been high before. Now I was smoking weed daily while working my summer job. Then it happened, one of the guys I was running with at the time introduced me to his "connect" (weed supplier). I began using money from my summer job to purchase weed, mostly to smoke and sell to make back the money I had spent. We called it "flipping" your money. It seemed like the best viable option, to be able to smoke for free and make your money back. I had no rational understanding that I was dealing drugs. So, I'd go to school to sell joints - rolled up weed, using thin white smoking papers, Zig Zag's - to my friends. I'd leave school . . . and come back later after-school gym and then hang some more until my curfew.

This repetitive behavior would continue until I was expelled for truancy and had to transfer to another school. I tried to find new things to do at the new school that were constructive. I went out for football trials during my sophomore year. But, without maintaining a 2.0 grade point average, I was cut from the team. Eventually, I quit playing sports my sophomore year and incidentally fathered a child, which ultimately was my reason for dropping out during my junior year.

Now, here I was just a kid myself about to become a father at 17 years of age. I'll never forget coming home, telling my mother that I was going to be a father. That was one of the scariest moments of my young adult life. Surprisingly, she was supportive; she told me I needed to get a job so that I could help support my child. I went out and found employment. I've always worked during the summer and participated in the work study program in school (a program that allows you to attend class for hours a day, then credits for working the other hours during school). Meaning, I was no longer in school; I needed a full-time job. Never really being forced to work, this was hardening. I only worked so that I would have money to squander with my friends and not have to ask my parents for anything. But now, it wasn't supposed to be about me, I had to take responsibility for another being and I was terrified to say the least.

The dead-end cycle was starting to take effect. I could never get to work on time as I was always partying with my friends. Finally, I was terminated again and continued this consequential pattern until I was in my early twenties. Similarly, being a total loser and a poor example of a father, I decided I needed to do something more positive with my life. With more irrational thinking, I decided to join the military. That's right! I, the one who had a blatant disregard for authority or rules, would seek refuge in a branch of the service. I went to a local recruiter and told them I was interested in enlisting. Of course, they sold me on all the benefits of joining and they would even help me obtain my General Equivalency Diploma (GED) and take me to the entrance exam. With that being said, I was all in.

The night before exams, which was scheduled for Saturday morning at 9 a.m., I went to hang out with my guys and celebrate. We drank and smoked like we always did because none of us had anything constructive happening in our lives. When you have a loser mentality, you surround yourself with people of the same mindset. Of course, they had the usual remarks unmotivated people make, such as "why do you want to go in the service, man? You won't make it." I didn't give much validity to those comments. I've always been mentally strong and determined once I made up my mind to do something. We continued drinking and smoking until the early hours of the morning. Needless to say, when the recruiter called at 9 a.m. to let me know he was on his way, I told him "give me until noon." When noon came, I ignored his calls. There was no way possible that I would be in any condition to take such a comprehensive cognitive examination. So, like everything else in my life, I blew that off as well.

Another season passes, I'm still between dead-end jobs and never present for my kid because I'm too busy running from and failing at being responsible. I had no idea what it meant to be a man and damn sure had no clue how to be a father.

Then one day I'm at home getting high, trying to map out a plan for my life, or should I say come up with another bright thought about what the next 5 or 10 years of my life would look like. Every day was the exact same as the day prior; absolutely nothing. Then, this commercial for "Job Corps of America" comes on the television. "Job Corps" was a National Technical Trade School. You could live on campus or reside at your home while studying for an occupational trade to assist you in making a livable wage. So, it hit me, Job Corps, would be my resource for a better life. Yeah, I'd finally figured it out now. I went to apply despite the program was located in another township within my state. I filled out the application and was all set to go live on campus. There I could learn a trade that would turn my life around. That meant I would be leaving my kid and returning to visit on the weekends, which, of course, made perfect sense to me. The program was 24 months long and, once I completed it, I'd be back at home able to provide for my child.

Well, a small form of rationality kicked in. I was doing better than imagined. I was attending classes; I even displayed some interest in the programs. I was actually feeling a sense of accomplishment and sticking it out.

As another season approached, with it came my biggest storm. I met a guy who was attending a business program at Job Corps. We hit it off instantly becoming friends. This friendship, unbeknownst to me, would have the greatest impact on my life. We would hang on campus during the week, then hang off campus on the weekends. During one of our weekends, he introduced me to his uncle. There was a sense of allurement. He had the appearance of someone who was successful. The problem was he was in 'the life' - hustling, selling drugs.

His style of life was very appealing to a young man's eye, the true epitome of a hustler, the cars, clothes, money, and an endless supply of spongers (people who hung around, groupies of the trade).

We went into his apartment; it was extremely lavish, dimly lit, smoky, and loud. It wasn't a party in the traditional sense. Yet, everyone seemed to have this fictitious enjoyment. I couldn't really put my finger on it, but nothing seemed real. There were boxes of brand-new items (TV's, VCR's, microwaves, and clothes everywhere). Most of which still had tags on them, indicating they were brand new.

I've always been introverted, that meant I was more observant whenever I entered a room full of people. Yet, there was something off about this introduction. Then I saw it. There on a table surrounded by 5 or 6 people, 'cocaine.' Prior to that, I'd only seen it in movies or heard it mentioned in songs. But here I was standing amongst the "den of thieves" (those who pushed for profit) while thumbing their noses at the working class in society. I didn't know what to make of it all at first. So, I just watched and laughed with everyone else. But, in the bedlam of my mind, I sensed this dark world would become intertwined within my own, bringing all that comes with it.

Later that week, my friend returned to campus and told me he was leaving his program. I asked why? He replied, "I can make way more money working for my uncle." First, it didn't register; he had so much going for himself. He was smart, with a good sense of direction for his life. He left that evening and I felt a pain inside. I thought I was losing a friend. I'd grown fond of the talks we shared and enjoyed hanging out together.

Nevertheless, he was moving onto a course to make some 'serious paper,' as we called it. Meanwhile, the rest of us would be here dreaming of the day we could afford to buy a car.

The weekend arrived, with a majority of us hanging out around the campus drinking and getting high, living the broke student life. While we were sitting around in our usual spot, my friend pulled up in a clean new ride, dressed in fresh gear, and seemed to have found his place in this world. We all laughed amazed at his return and going from rags to riches. He shared some of his stories of his newfound success. Then, he pulled out a bank roll (large amount of cash) to substantiate his proclaimed success. See, in 'the life' you couldn't just talk about it, you had to show and prove, and he was definitely catching my eye. He asked me to take a ride. As we were riding, my mind would drift. This was exactly what I wanted for myself. He told me his uncle liked me and wanted me to come work for him. At first, I thought he was just talking, or it was the weed. But then he handed me some money and told me to meet him next weekend. We rode a little longer; the smell of fresh leather from the new car filled the air. The sounds of our favorite jams coming through the speakers captivating my mind.

We connected that following weekend and went to his uncle's residence. I learned how to bag up (putting drugs into packages to be sold) and listened to his uncle's analogy on how to make money hustling. Every hustler has a psychological approach to handling his or her operation. He spoke of loyalty, trust, and never snitching which, is totally ironic in a game of deception.

You learn early not to disrupt the flow or go against the grain. That night, when we were done, I was paid 300 dollars which was more than I received in three months in my program at Job Corps. From that moment on, money became my passion. Something else also transpired that evening. It was the second turn of my irrational thought process. I could never see that because the money became my motivation, my "God" in a sense. I chased it from that day forward like a junkie person strung out on drugs- needing a fix.

My fluctuation between bouts of rational thinking and irrational behaviors allowed me to complete my program, gain a job, and sell drugs after work hours. Total loser, nothing seemed off with this approach I had dreamed up. It would give me the best of both worlds. In my mind, I knew I had to account for the money and what more logical way than to work a job. Yeah, I was a real sharpshooter.

I continued selling drugs after work, being absent from my kid's life, and moving in the most dangerous arena I've ever encountered.

A few more seasons would pass; things were rolling along pretty good. My friend and I were making money, and I was starting to see the potential of securing more financial resources. Consequently, we had our first encounter with law enforcement. The spot that we used to sell drugs was raided and my friend was arrested and charged with third degree sales of a controlled substance. I was cited for being in a disorderly house and released. We hadn't planned on getting busted; there was no methodology for this inevitable occurrence. My friend would ultimately be faced with prison or, if he was lucky, probation because he had no prior criminal history. Me, on the other hand, I was straddling the fence. Since I was only charged with a misdemeanor citation, I wasn't sure I wanted to stop selling drugs. I'd just have to re-route and find another source of supply.

I remember going to see my friend after he was released; we sat there talking. I could see the fear of uncertainty in his eyes, the concern for his family, and the fact he was about to become a father. Unlike myself, becoming a father had given him a purpose to do something different and make a change in his life. I saw being a father as a responsibility, rather than the privilege he discovered; I would discover this, years later.

Fortunately, he received probation, landed a decent job, bought a home, and got married. A true and complete change had occurred in his life, and he took full advantage of the opportunity for a second chance.

One day while driving around, which is something I did often, with no destination, just riding, I stopped by my friend's new home. It had been quite some time since we had last spoken. I noticed he had a glow. There were a couple of his new friends there. They were having a family get-together. I remember feeling so out of place. Here my friend was, living a real life with his family, and I was full-fledged in the street life.

So, I stood around feeling out of place, with a friend whom I had become estranged with, making small talk, and since we no longer moved in the same circles, we had nothing in common. Remember, loser gravitate to losers, and he had clearly found a greater purpose for his life. I knew it was time to say our final goodbye. As I reflected back on the drive from his home, once more, a feeling of envy surfaced within me. I now wanted what he had, but I was clueless on how to obtain it.

CHAPTER TWO

Consequences

A few more seasons would pass; I fathered two more children. Although I was there financially, I was both physically and emotionally absent. I still lacked the maturity to be a father.

Then my fate would come to fruition. It was June 27, 1991, my mother's birthday. I was in charge of her celebratory dinner. I was supposed to pick up the potato salad from my aunt, then return to my mother's home to help set up for the 4 p.m. celebration. However, when you live in the fast lane, you seldom allow a day for just relaxation. It's always money first. So, I answered a call just like any other day, met a customer, and set up a deal. I would meet with this guy in route to my mother's party, which proved to be a fatal mistake on my part. Arriving at the meeting spot for a simple swap, cash for drugs, and then I am out and on my way to the party with plenty of time to spare.

Upon arrival, the buyer approached me, showed the money then gave a discreet signal to law enforcement. They swarmed me, guns drawn, yelling commands. It was happening in real time, but everything seemed to be in slow motion. The indescribable adrenaline rushed through my body; my body's hormonal response kicking in 100 miles per hour All I heard was the yelling, which all seemed surreal, and the foggy thoughts running through my mind. What felt like a dream, or a nightmare, was actually reality. I was arrested on my mother's birthday for possession with intent to distribute "cocaine and cocaine base" (commonly known as crack). See, it was real and the guys wearing the blue and yellow windbreakers were none other than the DEA (Drug Enforcement Agency). I had finally made a full spectacle of my life, arrested on my mother's special day while she awaited my arrival with her potato salad for the host of friends and family expected to attend. Absolute loser.

Riding in the back of that squad car, I wasn't registering the severity of the situation. I was hoping like hell I could get out before my mother realized what happened. Not a chance of that ever happening.

I was taken to the county jail and processed. I remember that long, grueling method, being held on probable cause of narcotics with the intent to distribute a controlled substance. The jailor's deputies handed me a bed roll (issued to inmates upon intake, usually a sheet, blanket, a toothbrush, and small tube of non-descriptive toothpaste). We then proceeded to a housing area where I'd be held until my first court appearance. I don't remember sleeping that night. People were coming in and out of the cell unit all night. Then around 5 a.m., they turned on the lights, called breakfast, and we were each given an apple and a cinnamon roll. Needless to say, I had no appetite for food. My mind was bleak and all I could think of was my mother.

At or about 8 a.m. that morning, the deputies called my name and told me to "roll 'em up" (term used to indicate you're leaving and to turn in the items given at intake). Excitedly, I headed to the large metal door where the guard stood with this insolent grin on his face. I remember the words he stated to me, "congratulations, you made it to the big leagues." Then, he asked me if "I had crossed state lines." I wasn't certain what he was implying. My confused look must have revealed that to him. He then told me the U.S. Marshals were there to pick me up to be arraigned in Federal Court that afternoon. Instantly, not only was I dumbfounded, but I had no inkling about the Federal Courts or their process. They took me across the street to the Federal Building that housed the Federal Court. I was then processed by the U.S. Marshals and held for a 1 p.m. court appearance. Time seemed to be standing still. It had been less than 24 hours since my initial arrest and now I was sitting in my second judicial holding facility awaiting my fate. 1 p.m. came, I was shackled both hands and feet, ushered into this massive courtroom. Vividly, I see this huge podium, presumably where the judge would sit. There were a few large, expansive tables. The room had a cold and effectual prudence about it.

I sat there awaiting the proceeding to begin. The bailiff called "All rise," and in walked this stoic-looking man in his black robe. I can still see his skeptical gaze staring into my face. The prosecutor read the charges and asked for specific bail requirements. Swiftly, the terms and conditions for bail were set. I was then released pending trial. What had seemed like years had actually taken place in 24 hours. Unbeknownst to me, the trajectory of my life would be forever impacted.

Hearing those words from the Judge "Bail granted," was like reconciliation. While I was uncertain of my future, I was satisfied just to walk out of that courtroom. Before I was released, I was interviewed by pre-trial services. Their department sets the terms and requirements of your conditional release pending trial. Walking out of the Federal Building was a relief, but I couldn't shake the despairing emotion that I felt. I had no idea where to begin. There were so many things I needed to do, however, none of them were more weighty than going to see my mother.

I arrived at my mother's house shortly after leaving court. Walking through the door was more terrifying than all of the events that had transpired in the last 36 hours. I remember the grave look on my mother's face, just before she broke down in tears. As she embraced me, shivering uncontrollably, all I could do was try to comfort her. I couldn't form the words to tell her I had been arrested. At that moment, she was just at ease knowing I was alive.

A few hours would pass as I told her about the events regarding my disappearance. The sullen look in my mother's eyes translated her disappointment; at the time I could sense her fear. Here we were, just hours after her celebration, discussing the probability of her only son going to prison.

There were so many intricate layers to be worked out. I had to retain legal representation and gain understanding of the government's case against me. So, I hired an attorney. We went over the government's initial complaint against me and the penalties regarding the alleged offense. I was informed we would be notified within the next 30 to 60 days once the government filed the indictment against me. Then we would have another hearing to plead guilty or not guilty and set a date for trial.

A few weeks passed. I received that dreaded call from my attorney. The government had indicted me on 3 separate felony counts. He set the hearing date and our consultation meeting to discuss the indictment in detail. The federal government operated by sentencing guidelines and these were referred to as mandatory, which meant for me, as the defendant, that I was looking at a lengthy prison sentence, even though I was a "first time offender." There was no deviation from those guidelines without cooperation. To summarize, I was screwed.

There's a moral protocol expected of those who live 'the life' and that means under no circumstances do you EVER cooperate with any law enforcement officer or agency. You take this solemn oath as a part of the underworld consortium and, by all means, I intended to live up to the code.

The summer came and went. I had a couple of court dates. We reviewed the government's discovery - the evidence against me - and I was prepared to go to trial. My guidelines were "120 to 151" months, less 54 days a year for good time conduct. I remember having the conversation with my mother; she cried hysterically. The week prior to us going to trial, there was a severe weather storm, which closed down everything for 3 days. During the closures, my attorney received an email from the U.S. Assistant Attorney who informed him of a one-time offer of leniency "without cooperation." This would dismiss Count 2 and 3 of the indictment and allow me to plead guilty to Count 1, receiving a guideline sentence of "78 to 97 months." Also, in the email, the government stated they would "slam me" if I were to lose at trial. My attorney informed me of the government's position; telling me I had 72 hours to agree or the deal was null and void.

When you're 23 years old, there's often not much logic in our mental frame of thinking. So, I turned to my mother who, of course, was the voice of all reasoning. She encouraged me to see the bigger picture and to ultimately take the deal.

On February 5, 1992, I entered a plea of guilty in a Federal Court of law for possession with the intent to distribute "Crack Cocaine," and was sentenced to serve 78 months in a Federal Correctional Facility. Thus, my journey into corrections began.

"Against All Odds"

I was taken into custody and transferred to the Bureau of Prison Detention Center to begin serving my sentence.

The first season in prison went by fairly quickly. I spent my time working out, getting adjusted. There were quite a few people whom I became acquainted with. You sort of build a "brother of the struggle" when you're doing time, men who are from different backgrounds, ethnicities, and beliefs, all going through the same apparent challenge of being incarcerated.

You do so much just try to forget about the outside life, which, for most of us, is our biggest obstacle. The constant longing for contact or communication with loved ones is forever present until you're released. But time moves the same inside as it does outside in the free world once you find a way to occupy your time, as well as your mind. The 'brothers' you forge alliances with help that transition. Some men work in prisons industry, others take classes. All in all, you do whatever occupies your mind and allows the time to keep moving forward. Without regimen or schedule, you become mentally embedded in quicksand, its strong hold pulling you under into a state of depression.

Seasons went by rather quickly. I decided to take some community college classes with a couple of my buddies. It would be my first time being in an academic environment since obtaining my GED. In my mind, I always thought only smart people went to college. But, surprisingly to me, I did okay. The classes I participated in stimulated a desire to assist in passing time. However, I didn't invest in the probability of them changing my life.

So, without any real emotional investment, I eventually stopped participating in classes. I was no closer to my release date. I had no ideal plans for my future. Time had done exactly its intended purpose; keep on moving.

My season finally arrived. I was released to a halfway house in my community, finally freed after 6 years of incarceration. I had no plans for my life other than to meet the requirements of supervised release (a term of supervision attached to the end of your prison sentence). My term was four years. Penologists have stated "you are the exact age psychologically and emotionally when you leave prison, as you were when you arrived to prison, if you make no improvements on your development."

Here I was, back in my old surroundings, associating with the same people who had forgotten about me during my incarceration. I still had the same 24-year-old mentality, although I was now 30 years of age. All I could think of was making up for lost time. I reconnected with my kids who were now older and longed for their father who was financially present again, but physically absent once again. Mentally I was all over the place.

I was working nights now; I had been fortunate enough to obtain a job with my felony background. It didn't pay much, but I didn't have a plan past getting free and doing whatever I wanted to now that I was conditionally freed.

Fortunately, I completed my community corrections placement and was transferred to start my supervised release. The probation officer assigned to my case appeared to be an ex-military type who was covertly assessing my behaviors. I had already begun to show cues of deception, but it really was my disregard for law enforcement and going to prison that only made it more prevalent. I had what's commonly known in the penal system as "convict mentality." I would go on many years with this hold on my belief system.

My discontent with law enforcement began to play out in stages. I was hanging out in the old neighborhood having these run-ins because of my affiliations, although I saw it as "us against the system." Those interactions with law enforcement, on top of my resurrection of my drug dealing endeavors, began to pour to the surface and I was full-blown back in the game.

I had established a couple of businesses with my cohorts, attempting to legitimize my illicit activities which were starting to gain more attention from the law. I had begun to make some strides financially and achieved some sense of accomplishment, compared to the struggles of a few seasons ago.

Remember, no matter the accomplishments, it would be short-lived as long as irrational thinking was present.

In October of 2000, just 3 and a half years from my release from federal prison, I was arrested and charged with possession with intent to distribute a controlled substance and felon in possession of a firearm during the commission of a felony. I had only 4 months of supervised release to complete. Loser. Failure again. Now my fate would be determined again by a court of law.

I would go on to fight within legal allowances. My ensuing battle would come to an end in the appellate courts in August of 2002. I was remanded into custody and sentenced to serve 84 months in a state correctional facility. Concurrently, I was sentenced to an 18-month violation of the federal side for my conduct while on federal supervision. Seemingly, I had dodged another major bullet, compared to the possible outcome.

Here I was again, trying to recall the mishaps that landed me back in prison. I never really challenged my thinking that led to the actions. When you miscue in the game, it's never your fault. To take responsibility would be an admission of your irrationality. Therefore, blame is seldom placed on oneself.

CHAPTER THREE

Seeds of Discontentment

"What you think becomes what you believe, what you believe determines how you behave. How you behave determines what you experience." Unknown Author

Here I was again, back on the inside, I'd once again have to find a way to pass the time. The yard never changes, only the faces. Some come and go, while others are in for the long ride.

It didn't take long for me to gain my bearings. I had a solid reputation and stood by my "convict code," which ensured that I would have minimal problems on the inside.

Familiarity resurfaced and the seasons began to pass. As I drew closer to my release, I'd often wonder what I would do once released. I never really placed any emphasis on making a plan. I was a hustler by nature and always had ideals that would possibly procure some financial resources. So, my reservations subsided, and I would let the cards fall where they land.

Finally, I was released on home confinement with very strict supervision stipulations which included scheduled itinerary, curfew, and random drug analysis screenings. This form of intense supervised release was 18 months long; then I'd be transferred to standard parole for the remainder of my sentence.

After being out a few weeks, I found a job. I was able to gain employment as a sales associate for an automobile dealership. I experienced some bouts of excitement. I think it was associated to the art of structuring the deal that seemingly captured my interest. The auto industry had its upsides, but it also had surreptitious angles as well. Surprisingly, I didn't care for that part of the system of sales. There was something that seems predatory and sought to take advantage of unsuspecting consumers in every area of the matter. Now, that might sound a little hypocritical coming from me considering I was a convicted drug dealer. But, as I stated earlier, there are moral stances and beliefs even in nefarious activities. Thus, this legalized form of deceit would weigh on me at times. Even though I can't explain it, the thoughts were underlying and caused my half-hearted effort at times.

During one of my sales consultations, I met a client who inspired me to pursue another area of interest, buying and selling investment properties. Considering I was always financially centered, it didn't require too much convincing.

So, interestingly enough, I met with her spouse, and he taught me a sales system within the housing sector. I was intrigued with the capital affluence, and we formed a partnership. I started seeking others to be venture capitalists in our groups. I began achieving some financial independence. This was right about the time of our first fuel hikes within the U.S. in 2006, which started to impact the auto industry. Needless to say, I left my job to pursue the opulent life I envisioned for my family and myself.

A couple of rewarding seasons had occurred before the crash of the housing market in 2008, and the economy was not well as I began experiencing financial crisis. Seemingly, I weathered that storm and shifted my energy into another passion of mine health and wellness. Decidedly, I returned to school and completed my certifications to pursue my interest in the fitness industry. My other idled investments would take a backseat to my latest aspirations. The reality . . . this was more irrational behavior.

During my first two years back home, I had fathered two more children, which would also require more financial responsibility. However, I was finally starting to show more maturity as a father. I was physically, emotionally, and financially present as much as time allowed.

The curses and the blessings of my decisions had always been tunnel vision. Once I'm locked on a project, I can't see anything else. That's always been problematic for me. My relentlessness would become my downfall. All the measures of my short-lived success would be by any means necessary.

Most of the investments I made were extremely volatile. I was playing for short-term high gains and like most things that were too good to be true, they were. Consequently, that required me to raise the stakes or lose it all. So, decidedly, I doubled down praying for a short-term well-paying return. Unfortunately, I started taking massive losses and felt as though I was spinning my wheels in my other investments. No matter where I turned, there was no ground to stand upon.

It was my seventh-year home, now I had to make a dire decision; returning to my coping mechanism, going back to something I'd found success in when I wasn't experiencing it elsewhere. Whatever it was, it was a habit that went on for much too long; longer than you'd think considering I knew first-hand the consequences associated with those actions. But, like every time before I'd rationalize and make it a means to an end. While I had sowed the seeds of discontentment, the improper planning and continual irrationality would bring about my demise.

On September 13, 2013, eight years after my release from State Prison, I was indicted by the U.S. Federal Government for conspiracy to distribute Cocaine and Cocaine Base, as well as intent to operate a drug organization. The seeds had come to harvest. I was facing a presumptive "life sentence" as a 3-time career offender.

All I could do was sit back in disbelief. The irrational choices, incessant behaviors, and discontentment with my life would effectuate the circumstances to be carried out.

I was granted a conditional release and placed on a GPS monitoring system until sentencing. I forfeited real estate, business, money, and the social standing I'd worked so hard to build over those 8 years while I was free. However, nothing would come close to the disappointment, anguish, and hurt my actions brought unto my family once again.

A year later, I would receive the harshest sentence to date. Nearly 17 years of imprisonment.

Each of us has a picture in our minds of our lives however vague, of what we would like to accomplish before we die. How close we get to attaining this goal becomes the measure for the quality of our lives. If it remains beyond reach, we grow resentful or resigned. If it's at least in part achieved, we experience a sense of happiness and satisfaction.

For the majority of people on this earth, life goals are simple; to survive and if possible, to live with a certain amount of comfort and dignity. But, as soon as the basic problems for survival are solved, merely having enough and comfort are no longer sufficient to make us content. New needs arise and are felt. New desires arise. With affluence and power come escalating expectations. As our level of wealth and comfort keeps increasing, the sense of wellbeing we hope to achieve recedes into the distance. These paradoxes of rising expectations suggest that improving the quality of life might be an insurmountable task.

My issues began so early on; I was so fixated on what I wanted to achieve that I ceased to derive pleasure from the presence of my life. Unfortunately, when this happens, all possibilities of contentment are forfeited. The truth is the root of our personal discontent is internal.

Each of us must untangle the roots of our ailments personally, looking within for our own power. Because the shield of our external solace that may or may not have worked in the past leads us here, the order of our beliefs that religion patriotism, ethnic transitions, or habits installed by social classes are no longer effective. There are increased number of people like me, who feel exposed to the harshness of the chaos in their lives.

For me, this ideal is a dramatic paradigm shift. It was easier to blame other people, conditioning, or conditions for my stagnant situations. But, in order to take control over my life, I had to start with being "responsible-able." Knowingly, I influence my circumstances, and this allows me to become sensitive, receptive, and responsive. My ultimate goal is to feel the joy of contentment and triumph over pain and displeasure, living to do more than just cope. There will be many seasons to carry out during this sentence, but I'm facing each day with resolve. The goal each day is to be proactive and less reactive.

CHAPTER FOUR

Choices

"Existence alone had never been enough for him; he had always wanted more. Perhaps it was only from the force of his desires that he regarded himself as a man to whom more was permitted than others." **Fyodor Dostoyevsky, Crime and Punishment**

From the moment I felt the cold shackles around my wrist, my mind began to start my fight or flight response. There was an indescribable sensation that created a panic within me, almost a sense of doom. It was at that exact moment that I began to wonder if I'd ever see freedom again.

During that transit ride -the bus ride to prison-, I was visualizing the remainder of my life flashing by. There were so many cars on the roads, just like any other day. Except, today wasn't a normal day for me. I could see the perfect hues of blue in the sky, the sun seemed unusually brighter that morning. School buses were transporting kids to school, there appeared to be hundreds, if not thousands, of people driving to work. It was commerce for the rest of the world. Unfortunately for me, my day was ill-fated, it was one of the most horrific days of my life.

Although I'd done a couple of bids (terms used for prison sentences), nothing could prepare me for the 202 months I was sentenced to serve in Federal Prison.

You never forget that first night in prison. There's an erratic silence in the depth of night behind those iron doors, a staleness that never dissipates. You'll spend every hour of each new day in the exact manner as the previous day. Your mind will be on auto-replay contemplating the severity of the sentence you just received.

I've never lived my life making excuses for my actions. I believed, like so many other young African American males trapped in a skewed thought process, "I was doing what I had to do." My barometer never registered anything different. The recurrences of my negative outcomes were the direct indicator of my flawed belief system. Yet, if you've never had to examine the content of your choices, then it would be next to impossible to create a belief system that could produce a different result. Most of this may or may not jive with your rational thought process. However, most deviants like myself operate on the opposite end of the spectrum. Our irrationality directs the emotions that creates the defeatist results.

Certainly, most people would argue, when you become of a certain age, you'd understand the difference between right and wrong. Which is true to a certain extent. The contrast being people who are "fundamentally irrational thinkers" respond to stress stimuli in a different capacity. Meaning, rational people operate and are aware of situations through introspection. And their efforts allow them, to some extent, to subtract emotions from their thinking and counteract their efforts.

Irrational people have no such awareness. They rush into action without carefully considering the ramifications and consequences. Rational people demonstrate over time that they are able to finish a project, to realize their goals, and work effectively within a system or a team. They also tend to create things that last. Irrational people review their lives in negative patterns - mistakes that keep repeating, unnecessary conflicts that follow them wherever they go, dreams and projects that are never realized, anger and desire for change that are never translated into concrete action. They are emotional, reactive, and unaware of this behavior.

Therefore, you can clearly see the framing when a man or woman doesn't have a plan for his or her life. Then, all of his or her intentions will be short-lived. They'll often drift through their lives without ever defining value within their lives.

In most cases, if you stayed broke and hungry long enough, your value system is bound to change. For me, the streets would become my refuge. Whatever your angle, your scam, or your hustle, 'the life' (term used to refer to those living nefarious activities) was there to help seal your fate.

In 'the life,' (meaning years spent hustling, selling drugs) those of us who walked along that dark and destructive path convinced ourselves that our fundamental irrational thinking would somehow produce a favorable outcome. This flawed mode of operation had caused me to believe I could change the conditions of my life, without any regard to the consequences in conjunction with my actions.

There is a very clear and distinct awareness in the power of thought. This can be exemplified in four components, two of which produce confirmation; these parts of our thoughts are invisible, and the other two components produce visible verification as to the authority our thoughts have over our lives. The first component being - our thoughts (which are invisible) drive our emotions (which are also invisible). Second - our emotions drive our actions (which are visible). Third - our actions drive our results (which are tangible). And fourth - most amazingly, our actions are based on our thoughts whether that thought is true or not. With that being said, nothing I chose to do would have ever had a positive sustaining outcome. Because my thoughts were flawed.

Most of my life had felt sort of dark, during different intervals. Sure, I experienced some remedial levels of achievement, even some tangible traces of momentary success, but it was always short-lived. I used the same dominant negative thought pattern and expected different results. Correspondently, if our thoughts are the driving force behind our choices, I seriously needed to re-evaluate my thinking. We know that impulsive behaviors are often linked to a more subterranean issue.

There are many arguments to be made regarding nature versus nurture, or absentee parental guidance, and environment. In spite of that, I'm merely trying to discover the reasoning behind my choices. In addition, I'm trying to find a link to less self-destructive thought patterns. We will look at our thought centers in an upcoming chapter. Aside from that, the best way to examine the unscrupulous preferences I've made, and that we all make sometimes, is through self-introspection (the process of concentrating on your own thoughts of feelings).

Many days I'd sit still, looking out the window in my cell, reflecting upon and thinking about my life. I was thinking about all the twists and turns you've read about thus far . . . the traumas, the poor decisions that brought me to this point in my life again. What had I done wrong? I thought about the actions that played a part in returning to prison for the third time. There were no fingers to be pointed, no blame to be shifted, and no matter the internal dialogue. I had come to terms with, "we are where we are in life because of our choices."

From that moment, I became centered on effecting the best possible outcome. Regardless of my current circumstances or situation or positioning of my life and expeditiously working on the mistakes and living within my current reality. My focus shifted to finding a constructive outlook on my past choices, and more importantly forgiving myself and seeking real change.

In my process of self-introspection, I needed to clean out the "junk in my box" (meaning: mental hang-ups, insecurities, grudges, and any unexamined negative emotions) that would impede my progress. I needed to start with a clean emotional slate by making amends where applicable and then move on. This personal inventory allowed me the opportunity to grow mentally and remove all grandiose attitudes and behaviors. It granted me empathy towards others. It also created a sincere desire for service or giving back. None of this was an easy process, requiring total honesty, and an unrelenting conviction daily; sometimes hourly. Yet today and every day moving forward, I've made an emotional, mental, and spiritual commitment to the journey of making rational choices in my life. I'm not waiting for a certain time to begin. I live each day with a renewed purpose. I'm conscious of the choices I make and the collateral impact my choices have on those I care about. I review my "plan of action" daily, making sure it coincides with my desired results.

These actions can be implemented in all areas of your personal life, as well as your professional endeavors. Maybe you're dissatisfied with your current job? You can evaluate the thoughts and choices you make daily continuing to work in a toxic environment. Or it could be a relationship or goals that you put off. Whatever the circumstances or situation, we should all take inventory of the "junk in our boxes."

We all face unique and individualized difficulties, and although there's no universal solution, the power of our thoughts will determine the results. It doesn't mean we will be free from making poor decisions. The difference I've found is my ability to live with the resolution of my actions surrounding the choices or decisions I've made . . . good or bad, no excuses, accepting responsibility and achieving the personal growth associated to the positive power of choice.

Once again, these were the tools that helped me; I hope you find them useful as well. They are not a guarantee. Notwithstanding – when you make healthy and positive choices, positive actions and results are sure to follow.

Everything is part of something bigger; mistakes or poor choices are no exception. Every minus is a half of a plus, waiting for a positive stroke of vertical awareness.

In the book of Illusions, Rich Bach explains that every problem comes with a gift in its hands. If you focus only on what went wrong, you miss the gifts. If you are willing to look deeper (self-introspection) and ask for insight, the problems dissipate. You are blessed with learning and advance on your path.

Remember, this isn't about being incarcerated, you can apply the components of thoughts or choices to every aspect of your life. Just start with the first step of cleaning out the junk in your boxes, or mental closets. Then plan, review it daily, make an emotional commitment to your process. By doing so, you'll be on your way to freedom of thought and choices.

Furthermore, through our mistakes, bad fortune, and loss we can choose to look for opportunity. Since everything is what you make it, you can create success by focusing on what has gone right, even when it seems to have gone wrong.

Today and every day, I encourage you to use every experience as a steppingstone to something greater. We all have a choice.

CHAPTER FIVE

Mirrors

"An unexamined life is not worth living"

~ Socrates

There are many commonalities in our lives, some of which we often identify with the same likeness in others. Most times we can mirror the good we see; other times we reflect those images in a negative capacity. More times than not, it becomes easier to recognize the good in someone else's life, rather than seeing the good in our own.

I remember growing up watching people who I believed at the time were a measure of true success, from all of their external material measurements. I drafted my view, and values, often emulating those images. Now, I'd be the first to admit that most of those characteristics were less than desirable. As you have read in the previous chapters, however, my value system was created around those false images which I deemed earlier on in my life as successful.

It was never easy to measure their failures because mentally I perceived they had no flaws or difficulties. I couldn't imagine with all the appearances of success they portrayed that their lives could be problematic.

Consequently, our lives can't be mirrored by the lives of people we know or see. There needs to be a clear understanding of what is the center of your life. I previously spoke of our centers in the forementioned chapter. Perhaps, the best way to identify with your center is to look closely at your life-support factors.

If we can identify with this concept, we can trace back to the center of where the thoughts flow and locate a center which may be limiting your personal effectiveness.

A person who mirrors beliefs, or actions, thoughts, and attitudes may be fluctuating from one center to another. The resulting relativism is like a rollercoaster. One moment you're high, the next moment you're low. Making efforts to compensate for one weakness by borrowing strength from another weakness. There is no consistent sense of direction, or sense of personal intrinsic worth nor identity. (Example: our favorite celebrities often give us glimpses inside their lives, and instantly we subconsciously mirror their external behaviors. The cars, the clothes, the jewelry, and lavishness of a life is what we dream to be more valuable than our own).

Our security comes from knowing that unlike other centers based on people or things which are subject to frequent and immediate change, our correctly centered principles within ourselves do not change; we can depend on them. The principles we develop, strengthen and rely on do not react to anything. They don't get mad and treat us differently. They won't divorce us and run away with our best friends. They aren't out to get us. They can't pave our way with shortcuts or quick fixes. Our true personal wellbeing doesn't depend on behaviors of others, the environment, or current fad for validity.

Admittedly, we're not omniscient. Our knowledge and understanding of correcting our lives is limited by our own lack of awareness and true measure of the world around us. We may be limited in our understanding, but we can push back the borders of our limitations.

By gaining greater understanding of our own personal value and self-worth, we can live with the confidence that the more we learn, the more clearly we can focus the lenses through which we see our lives, the lives of others, and the world around us.

The themes I discovered and speak of in this chapter helped me to clearly define what I wanted in my life, giving me access to visions of a better life beyond the material realm.

I'd spent the earlier years of my life without a plan or vision for my success. I shaped my beliefs based on my thoughts without a clear understanding of what the actual center of my life was.

Fatherhood at a young age had given me responsibility, but I lacked the purpose to be gained, versus the hardship I associated to being a parent. My mother, in her teenage years, did the best she could with the limited opportunity she had. I was doing the opposite, having no real sense of purpose for the opportunities I was fortunate to experience. Subsequently, I settled for the shortcuts in life. I have used these tools to gain a better sense of self and to help you, the reader, obtain a potential template for identifying your personal centers.

See examples of (centers which shape and mold our lives). Recognizing your centers: (Reference, Behavioral Statistic Manual 1952).

Money-Centered: If your personal worth is determined by your net worth, you are money-centered

Work-Centered: If you are work-centered, you tend to define yourself by your occupational role.

Possession-Centered: If you are possession-centered, your security is based on your reputation, your social status, or tangible things you possess.

Pleasure-Centered: If you are pleasure centered, you feel security only when you're on a pleasure high.

Friend-Centered: If you are friend-centered, your security is a function of the social mirror.

Enemy-Centered: If you are enemy-centered, your security is volatile, based on the movement of your enemy.

Church-Centered: If you are church-centered, your security is based on church activity and on the esteem in which you are held by those in authority or influence of the church.

Self-Centered: If you are self-centered, your security
                        is constantly changing and shifting.

The above appendix of recognizing your center is not a
measurement to be used as judgment tools. You may find
relevance in one or more areas as I have in my personal
reflections. However, we can use the aforementioned
information as a tool for personal awareness, to assist in
finding contentment in our daily lives or space regardless of
circumstances or situations.

CHAPTER SIX

Clarity

"Change your thoughts and you change your world."

~ **Norman Vincent Peale**

In order to change ourselves effectively, we must first change our perceptions. I had to delve into my thought process and evaluate why I consistently participated in actions that were detrimental to my wellbeing. I needed to define clarity and to assess my capacity to apply the findings of my observation. Then, I needed to determine which pathway would produce better results in my life.

Clarity is defined as notable precision of thought or expression, a decipherability. The more introspection I did, the more consciousness and clarity I attained. It became apparent how irrational my thought process factually was. The belief that I could change my conditions with no regard for the consequences associated to these actions was irrational.

It would take countless hours to embrace beyond my rationalizing and deflecting those past behaviors. There were things I did daily to invoke change of my perception. One, I started seeking information that was outside my closed mindset. Secondly, I vowed to become a lifelong learner to avoid stagnation of my personal growth. Most importantly, I began each day viewing my prosperity plan for my life. I declared a positive mind state and did the little things consistently to ensure I was accountable for my actions and potential consequences of those actions.

Through the paradigm shift of my perception, my mindset has begun to expand, thus allowing me to continually work for a personal change. However, it wasn't until I sought clarity and defined how having a greater understanding could possibly change the trajectory of my life.

Society portrays black people as the face of poverty, crime, and dysfunction. Basically, we are hard-wired not to expect too much from life, and consequently not to want much. We're taught early on the lessons that drive our thoughts and emotions. Our communities are labeled as good or bad, in areas where people of color see no beauty. Urban areas often display youth and adults sitting around drinking, smoking weed, selling drugs, toting pistols, or extreme violence. All of these loathsome behaviors shape the vision of our existence and lead many of us to lack hope. A lack of hope is an inner-city epidemic. Nothing holds a person back more than that.

Since so many young African American males are taught early on to go to school and get a good job, we become trapped in a vicious cycle and spend many years trying to achieve an illusion of prosperity. We've already bought into the idea that there's nothing greater for you or your life based on society's measure of success or failure.

In short, some of us simply give up and settle for less. That's exactly what transpired in my personal life, time and time again. I had no personal value or a perception that life could offer me something greater if I stayed the course and put in the hard work.

Perceptions offer us a chance to look at our lives or circumstances or situation through our lenses. We must ask ourselves the thought-provoking questions and seek honest answers, not just telling ourselves what we need to believe for justification of actions or inactions. We must do this often if we are to gain clarity. Questions like, how does my personal perception govern what I see? And how will my perception allow me to see how my behavior could possibly harm myself and others? It's also imperative to surround yourself with people who desire better for our wellbeing . . . mentally, emotionally and spiritually.

During my darkest moments, I depended unconsciously on the inner strength that resided in the depths of my core. There were moments lying in the gloom of my cell, my mind began to envision each brick in the wall as a ladder. Each step of this ladder would elevate my mind above and beyond the walls and fences that held me captive. It was there inside my cell I was forced to plan; call it my recognition for capacity to change. I was faced with a highly complex situation. Continue the vicious self-destructive thought patterns and behaviors that made me a 'three times loser,' or arm myself with the necessary psychological and intellectual capacity to ensure change. I chose the latter. The contemplation of my life in this secluded place had finally freed me mentally and given me the needed power for such a transformation to take place. If I hadn't sought clarity and experienced the paradigm shift, I would never have been able to change my reality. Therefore, not only would I be physically confined, but mentally as well. Which, ultimately, is a slow death. Like all living things, the mind needs nourishment to grow, or it becomes incapacitated and diminishes.

Change, real change, comes from the inside out. It doesn't come from hacking at the limbs of our attitudes and behaviors. Those actions are temporary at best and offer no long-term benefits.

If we are to form durable causation, we must realize there are no quick fixes of personality adjustments. It comes from striking at the root of our thought process. By giving definition to our character, we're able to create a broader lens through which we see the world.

My views of society had always been myopic. In medical terms, it is referred to as "a vision impairment of short sightedness," thus disallowing any perception of the future outcome.

Many of us live with the same blinding views on our careers, relationships, and goals. This is mostly derived from an instant gratification standpoint, where we see ourselves now, and "I want what I want now," regardless of if it may be hazardous toward our wellbeing years to come.

I quote Emerson: "That which we persist in doing becomes easier... not the nature of the task has changed but our ability to do has increased."

By centering our lives on correct focus and finding balance, we gain the ability to do what we want. We become empowered in the task of creating effective, useful, and peaceful lives for ourselves and our prosperity.

So, how can we reach this elusive goal that cannot be attained by a direct route? I'm convinced that the path begins with achieving control over the contents of our lives through our perceptions.

Our perceptions about our lives are the outcome of many that shape experiences, each having impact on whether we feel good or bad. Most of these forces are outside our control. For example – there's not much we can do about our looks and our temperament. We cannot decide – at least so far – how tall we grow; how smart our children will get. We cannot choose parents nor siblings. However, working within ourselves and making a conscious effort will affect our perceptions, rendering clarity amongst chaos in our daily lives.

When we focus on our inner perceptions and remove the strength from the innumerable external conditions that impair our understanding, we then quiet the distractions. This allows us to work through discomforts of trauma, pain and ailments in order to challenge and expand ourselves.

As I explained in the previous chapters, publications cannot give us the recipes on how to be happy or joyful. Our optimal experiences depend on our ability to control what happens in the consciousness of our minds, moment by moment. Each person has to achieve it on the basis of his or her individual effort.

However, we are certain that establishing clarity opens our minds to the examples of how life can be more enjoyable in the framework of theory. As you examine your conclusions to achieving mental clarity, keep an open mind and trust in your process of becoming greater than your experiences.

In conclusion, remember most of us have spent years storing useless junk in our "mental boxes." It is essential to unpack and remove the trash we've collected if we are to achieve true clarity. See you in the next chapter!

CHAPTER SEVEN

Getting Out of Your Way

"When you've reached your bottom, there's nowhere left

to go but up"

~ Author Unknown

Wow! This chapter was so reflective for me. Here I was sitting in prison for the third time, one would think I would've learned from the two previous encounters. Yet seemingly, some things are more complex than the visible make-up. For me, getting out of my own way was the building that landed on top of me. Obviously, this is not in the literal sense, rather the psychological realization. Have you ever experienced a situation in your life where you thought, "God, I should've seen that coming?" Well, that's exactly what I'm reminiscent of.

I'd spent decades of my life incarcerated and continuously failed to see the dominant negative thought patterns that created the same results in my life. I had become the poster child for the definition of insanity: "

Doing the same things over and over and expecting different results." Indeterminately, all the factors I associated to my failures weren't responsible at all . . . not the people who snitched on me, or the law enforcement agencies that investigated the nefarious activities I had committed. No! It was me. I had always been standing in my way of any significant success. Honestly speaking, most of my difficulties felt quite normal to me. In the environment I lived in, most of the people had the exact same mind state; we were all trying to survive by any means necessary. We were all in survival mode.

I had always believed that life simply held out for those who were privileged and entitled to the amenities of life, amenities that people in my community could only dream of. However, nothing could've been further from the truth. The fact is you get out of life what you put in. As I mentioned in Chapter Four, "we are exactly where we are because of our choices." Although, that may have been hard for me to comprehend then, it doesn't negate the factual premise. The high achievers are willing to work hard, set goals, and have unwavering grit. It's impossible to see all the hard work someone else puts into their visions and goals. We can only measure the tangible evidence. My lack of sustainability was due largely to my failure to make a viable plan for my life. I had countless ideas and many failed attempts, but never a solid goal or vision for my personal success. And that is exactly what the content of your life becomes, your success and failures are yours alone. No one can be attributed to either, except you.

So, after decades of failing to live up to my fullest potential, I finally realized I had to get out of my way. See, I never had a problem of doing things, as you can clearly see. My quandary was I had an implementation problem. I failed to commit to anything substantial. Sure, I had some business ventures, earned some revenues, and had some perceptibility of success. However, there was no real emotional connectivity to drive any real potential prosperity. It's not enough to just want to do something or just do it. The things that add value to your life are the things you are emotionally invested in. Certainly, we all want a lavish lifestyle or to retire and live leisurely. Nevertheless, there could be something inside you that is holding you back. Have you ever had that feeling where there is a necessity within hungering for more? Yet, you can't quite figure out what it is all about. Well, you could be standing in your way as well.

Now, I'm not referring to discontent as mentioned in Chapter Three. Rather, I'm examining if there's a yearning for a higher purpose within. That's what I discovered in my life, a real hunger for a higher purpose. And, in order to achieve that goal, I had to defeat the dominant negative thought patterns that held me captive long before I was ever incarcerated. I had to remove the idealism of fear, inadequacy, and procrastination. Remember in the previous chapter I stated, "there's no illustration of how many times we must go through similar consequences to get to that point of growth." We simply start at the beginning and identify the obstacles that prevent us from living a purposeful life.

My personal steps were starting from where I was now, taking a mental inventory of my life, and using that process to help heal my past traumas. I had to seek clarity and understanding, making sure to unpack the baggage of past associative traumas as well. Meaning, not just the direct-related trauma, but also traumas associated to collateral actions of others as well. And I would do this every six month to ensure I evaluate any unseen or unforgiven areas of pain in my life. Through introspection, wellness, and meditation I've been able to help myself and continue moving forward. I work really hard not to let mistakes define my outcomes. An old instructor once shared some invaluable wisdom with me, and I'll gladly share it with you. He told me, "the clutter around us is a direct reflect of the clutter within." So, I try to spend time weekly, if need be, cleaning out the junk in the trunk of my mind. It has taken me many years to grasp that analogy, but with time comes wisdom and each day we should work to discover our best self.

In my process of getting out of my way, I created a prosperity plan for my life which gives me a visual reference to access the vision of my life, and what it looks like beyond the material realm. I have worked really hard to reshape my belief system and focus on a positive thought process. I no longer just have ideals; rather now I take the time to write down the realistic goals I set for myself, both intermediate and long-term. I focus daily on the needed tasks to achieving my goals. Also, I make sure to list potential obstacles, as well as my capacity to complete them. Lastly, I identify the pathway to my desired outcome. I complete these tasks daily to ensure consistency and that I remain focused on the now, regardless of my current circumstances. These are some of the steps I've taken to assure I'm no longer standing in my way.

In the book of "The Laws of Human Nature" by Robert Greene, he references our nature to animals; however, humans lack the insight and instincts to guide themselves past danger. We have to rely on our conscious ability to make decisions. We do it best in our career paths and handling the inevitable setbacks of life. But, in the back of our minds we can sense a lack of direction, as we are pulled this way and that way by our moods and by opinions of others. He describes that such drifting leads to dead ends. The way to avoid such a fate is to develop a sense of purpose, discovering our calling in life and using the knowledge to guide our decisions. In doing so, we come to know ourselves more deeply, our taste, and inclinations. We learn to trust ourselves, knowing which battles and detours to avoid. Even our moments of doubt and our failures have a purpose - to toughen us up. With energy and direction, our actions will have unstoppable force. It is my sincere desire that you, the reader, find the path that ensures you are no longer standing in your way. See you in the next chapter!

CHAPTER EIGHT

Fear

"You are the only real obstacle in your path to a fulfilling life."

L
e
s

B
r
o
w
n

In Chapter Seven, "Getting Out of Your Own Way," I shared one of the prohibiting factors that stagnated my personal development. "Fear." Actually, it is one of the most powerful emotions of the human psyche. It has the ability to take us into a hyper-dynamic mode of operating, or it can handicap us to a debilitating psychological moment.

I always considered myself to be somewhat fearless. I had spent the majority of my adult life taking life and death risks without much regard. I never saw or visualized myself as a fearful person. But fear isn't something we can see visually. No male wants to admit that he is afraid. So, it becomes this sudden predominate factor upon which we limit or shortchange our fullest human potential.

Growing up in my neighborhood, the last thing you wanted to project was fear. The bullies and parasites feasted on the passive and the weak. Society has disguised its views concerning masculinity. Even as a boy, I was taught not to cry or show weakness. Everyone knew boys in the hood don't cry. This created a false bravado concerning projected strength and identifiable weakness.

However, fear is more complex than the stereotypical tales of how boys or males behave. Fear creates a false picture of the world, piling on things to be afraid of that are in fact harmless. The mind adds fear. If the mind can undo the perception of fear, the danger will vanish.

To begin with, life cannot exist without fear. The two aspects, one positive, the other negative, meet inside your mind and determines the course of outcome.

There is always going to be something to be afraid of, a new worry or threat. However, our focus is not to be paralyzed from the fears. Rather, find the solution to overcome the fear that paralyzes us and leaves us stuck.

Sometimes, the problem is simpler than it may appear. Some of the things we worried about two years ago, five years ago, ten years ago, all worked out, and they will this time too.

There were many reasons why fear was controlling me. I became stuck in a self-destructive pattern. To break out of that mindset, I learned to over-ride my fear. By creating an emerging awareness that says, "the fear isn't real; I'm the one creating it." This allowed me to become aware of my self-induced fear.

Fear can be one of the most convincing emotions of all, in part because evolution has hardwired the brain to react with the fight-or-flight response. It's that feeling of your heart racing that tells you in no uncertain terms what you must do. But the voice of fear isn't telling you the truth. It is using the power to convince you, even when you have nothing to be afraid of.

The tool of detachment from your thoughts of fear has the ability to help you heal in these cases. If you can say to your fear, "I don't believe in you, I don't accept you," its power to convince you will diminish.

Once we begin to dismantle the physiological impact fear has on us, we can create the lives we envision for ourselves. The power of positive thought enables us to move forward, sending a message to our fears that we will not be victimized. We are no longer running away from our visions, rather we run toward them. Say "I can face fear and still do things that scare me." When you take this stance, you regain control and your fears vanish.

From this we've learned fear is always a projection of the mind into the future. If we examine our fears, they have nothing to do with what is happening now. Ask yourself, what do I fear? And is my fear limiting me from achieving my visions and goals? Finally, what do I need to do to regain control over those thoughts?

Our fears generally tend to be about bad things that might happen. If something happened that was threatening to your wellbeing, you, like me, would be guided as to what to do in that moment without thinking about it much or feeling afraid. You just have to let your conscious thought of wellbeing take over and disallow fear to control your thoughts.

The sole purpose is to believe we are more capable of achieving our vision. We are more than worthy of the good things we desire for ourselves. We must disallow any negative thoughts, emotions, or actions that hinder our growth.

"I am protected by wise guidance deep within me.
I need not fear." Anonymous

~

CHAPTER NINE

Still, Stuck, Stopped

"Aspirations & inspirations evolve into ambition

unknown

While writing this chapter, I've contemplated the dynamics: still, stuck and stopped. I have often reflected on situations and occurrences and the times in my life where these stages were defining, as well as limiting my personal growth.

Full comprehension of the depths of each phase required me to search internally and ask some thought provoking questions. For example, 'where was I during each phase? How did I react during these periods in my life?' Furthermore, 'what were the results associated with the actions?'

In order for us to achieve our fullest potential, we must thoroughly understand ourselves and the obstacles that hinder us mentally. If our thoughts drive our emotions and our emotions trigger the actions, our actions drive our results. Then, we are obligated to closely analyze our thoughts.

I had spent most of my life surviving, never establishing the freedom to thrive. I had countless jobs that were nothing more than a paycheck. Each Monday I was back to the exact feelings of being miserable at the thought of a new work week.

Have you ever felt trapped in your day-to-day living? I'm sure most of you can relate to the restlessness of my actions. Time just seemed to pass by on most days; each day revealing nothing greater than the day before.

Ironically, I was imprisoned long before I ever served my first prison term. I wasn't invested in my future, and I had no realistic goals. I had some opportunities earlier on in my life, but I lacked the discipline to accomplish the tasks. It was really challenging for me to exude the needed patience. I was discouraged after watching people I knew working two jobs, and seemingly having very little to show for it. I guess my false entitlement played the largest part in my thought process. However, I just couldn't rationalize the value of honest work. So, my attraction to the familiarity of projected success in my community became my focal point.

It wasn't until my first prison sentence that I actually had to be still in my adult life. My life always seemed to be moving a hundred miles an hour, but now there was no more hustling and moving fast. For me, I couldn't decipher which was worse, the fact I had lost my freedom or the thoughts of not being able to do exactly what I wanted to do. I'd always played by my rules and now I was under the scrutiny of a higher authority. It might be hard to consider but being confined was more of a challenge to me.

It was at that point that I began to examine the totality of my situation. I had to reconnoiter the mind state of the 24-year-old male who had no real sense of self, and no concise directions for his life at that point.

When I started writing about my journey and examining different periods of my life, I was able to draw reference to the mentality I demonstrated during those phases and I could ascertain the significance of the power of thought. Thus, I was able to clarify and recognize the meditative ability to measure the impact of each phase. I referred to the phases: stuck and stopped.

Although it had taken me years to gain perspective and understanding to be able to identify associative traumas I've experienced through the years, I am elated to share my personal discovery during these phases in my life.

Webster's dictionary gives us a base interpretation, meaning, an ostensible relation. However, we're going to look in-depth, create a paradigm in the thought process as it relates to each phase in our personal journeys.

Still: Deep, quiet calm. Not moving – The first phase was actually quite shocking to me. My whole life had been one big hurry-up movement. I had to acquire and achieve in order to feel stable in my life. Well, with that sense of hurriedness, I'd always fail to create a calm or inner peace in my life. I couldn't stand to be left alone with just my thoughts. It felt too isolated, oftentimes leading me to surroundings that felt even emptier; even though the room would be filled with people.

It has taken years of introspection to establish acceptance and a sense of fulfillment in a calm state. This realization overturned the belief that life can't be satisfying every waking moment regardless of circumstances. For me, I just had to allow the process to be natural and effortless. Have you ever been in a position in your life where you just couldn't seem to embrace the still moments?

Perception isn't hard to shift. The actual enlightenment is similar to that aha! moment we all experience. Everyone has an awakening period; the challenge comes with learning to be receptive and trusting in your process. There are many degrees of enlightenment, as well as different time periods. Most of my trials were the redefining moments for me. However, you never know what the burst of insight will be in your lives. Just be willing to embrace the divine process or sense of a higher power within the universe at work in your life. In that calmness you can achieve the knowledge that works for your greater good. Allow yourself to examine and reverse your limiting thoughts that the universe is empty and impersonal; know you are always cared for.

The greatest part is the shift in perception|: waking up each day and facing your period of "still."

Stuck: past participle of stick; to become stopped or delayed; come to a standstill.

This was one of the most troubling phases for me. As I drifted from situation to situation, I was mentally trapped. I had become a master of surviving, but it was virtually impossible for me to reach that level where I was thriving in my life. There was no apparent solution that would seem to change my circumstances. No matter the attempt, most of my efforts were short-lived.

This brought about the discontentment that plagued me mentally and caused this phase to persist and bring about continued catastrophic outcomes. For me, the feeling of being stuck was almost unbearable. Have you ever dealt with obstacles in your life that seemingly never dissipate no matter the effort that you put forth? Here I was doing what I believed at that time was my best, but to no avail would change come. It was during this phase that I made a conscious decision to do anything necessary to force a change, or my desired outcome. Taking on the belief by any means only led to greater despair. I would later discover how to effect change and bring about the desired outcome. However, during this mental period of being psychologically trapped, I was unable to grasp the needed fortitude to create a real change in my life.

Many years later, I discovered the process to dispose of the negative thought process that kept me stagnant and unable to achieve my goals and instead create a fulfilling plan for my life. Once again, it revolved around my thought process. We cannot build the lives we envision for ourselves until we remove all the mental roadblocks that hinder our personal growth. Fundamental irrationality was my greatest barrier. It has taken many years and several failed attempts to rid myself of this debilitating condition. It is no easy task to search within ourselves and make honest admissions to our inadequacies. However, if we are to manifest growth and reach our fullest human potential, then we must invest 100% of our efforts to maximize the compensation we envision. Is the life you are living what you envisioned for yourself? Are you in a situation where you feel stuck or at a standstill in your life? Then, I encourage you to challenge your thinking. Examine the limiting thoughts or fears that may be holding you captive.

By understanding our thought process, we can utilize the means to achieve our personal growth. We begin to comprehend and acknowledge the part we play in our positioning in life. We know we are where we are because of our choices. These choices are a direct correlation to our thoughts, both conscious as well as subconscious. There's much to be associated with the responsibility of taking the first step, and then examining which of your thoughts are hampering your goals or desired outcomes.

Once I acknowledged the part I played in my own demise, I became grateful for the hardships during those moments.

They became the catalyst that inspired my perceptions and belief system to change. It's because of these challenges in my personal life that I choose to share my testimony.

For me, the feeling of being stuck is no longer a hindrance in my life. I have a hindrance that disallows my pain and suffering to be an excuse.

Today in my life, regardless of the circumstances or location, I have set realistic goals that are interim as well as short and long-term. I realize enlightenment is about total transformation, but not instant transformation. It's about being good in any space or situation. When you can validate your experiences, whether good or bad, whether mistakes and poor choices, then you become free to move forward. You are no longer the views of your life. You are living your life; you are no longer stuck.

Stopped: To cause a cease in motion, to keep a person from doing.

Unlike the latter phases, this phase became a daily challenge largely due to my current state. While I'm not physically free to pursue my goals and visions, I don't waste time complaining or being lazed. Initially, I was most affected during my pre-sentencing stage. Here I was once again with my life placed on pause, and my failures being viewed by all. It never mattered what others thought, but this time I felt an unequaled sense of loss. However, mentally I had to find a way to keep moving forward.

I recalled a conversation I had with my attorney after we discussed the possible sentencing guidelines. He stated, "this was viewed as a human failure." Now, I'd served two prior prison sentences, but I never viewed my mistakes as human failure. Immediately, I was taken aback I didn't react to his comment; I was more contemplative. But once I was at home it hit me. I was exactly what I never viewed myself as, a loser. I always thought in order to lose you had to actually give up, and that was something I would never do.

Ever since I was a child, I hated to lose; my competitive spirit was soaring long before I understood how to channel that energy in a constructive way.

The only time I'd ever experienced the emotional contingency was when I was incarcerated. My life always seemed to be stopped, and once I was released mentally, I was trying to make up for lost time.

With the uncertainty of my fate looming, I needed to distinguish what it meant to fail. I don't know why that was so important, because I couldn't undo any of the past events that had transpired. But the fact remained it's what I needed mentally. So, I actually looked up the word <u>failure</u>; the act, state, or fact of failing, not succeeding in doing or becoming. I called my attorney and I told him regarding our conversation of human failure, I realized you cannot fail at your attempts whether you win or lose. You only fail when you give up. I told him "I was the exact opposite; I never knew when or how to give up." It was from that moment on I would do everything within my power to become greater than all of my perceived failed attempts.

It was from that moment on I vowed never to lead a life that leads to self-destruction and inflicts harm to others. I was determined not to be handicapped by my circumstances. I would continue to grow, learn, and give back. With that frame of thought I could never be stopped. Situations don't define us; obstacles don't define us. We are defined by our faith, beliefs, and tenacity.

The phase of 'stopped' occurs only in your mind. There may be barriers that exist or limit your ability to prevail, but they only grow power if you subside mentally and lie down. It's okay to be sad or saddened or grief-stricken. We just can't afford to dwell there. For me, the power is only lost when I give up. There's no place on earth that you can place me, that I'll allow my spirit, will, or determination to falter. I am determined to soar, and my heart will give out before I ever give up.

There's a list of historic heroes that have risen from the "belly of the beast," slavery, incarceration, and physical disabilities. They have never allowed those storms of life to stop them. Some of the greatest "African-American Influencers" have come from being incarcerated, Malcom X, Mohammed Ali, Nelson Mandela, and Afeni Shakur. The list goes on and on. Just think of the great inspiration the world would've been denied if any of the greats would have been stopped because of circumstances.

I use those before me as my inspiration and guide today helping me to gain understanding that I am more than what happens to me. Their works become my aspiration. I can become what I choose to practice hourly, daily, and weekly. Allowing those triumphs from tragedy to be my source of "I can," so long as I choose to.

We must always look to be cautious to the power we give over us, even the simplest of things such as vocabulary can reign supreme.

Today and every day, I am conscious of the power of my thoughts and my words. Be free to enjoy the gifts of each new day, making the most of it. No one can stop you, but you.

CHAPTER TEN

Good, Better, Best

"Wanting something is not enough. You must hunger for it."

Growing up I felt very misunderstood. The caregivers in my life had their interpretations of my actions and behaviors. Often, they just could not rationalize my conduct. They did their best with being authoritative, loving, and supportive. However, they had failed to realize that I just didn't view things similar to my peers – other children my age. At a very early age, I would discover being disconnected and uninterested in the normal adolescent amusement.

There always seemed to be an extraordinary level of curiosity looming within me. I fully understand that all children are innately curious. This is part of our development. I was still considered to be outside the realm of societal "normal child standard." Looking back, my inquisitive nature was culminating. Unbeknownst to me, that spirit which dwelled within me would become the curse, but also the blessing in my latter years.

"Against All Odds"

This is a reflective deconstruction of my personal milestone – the above-mentioned latter years. I'll share a . . . devised manifest to becoming "self-aware," the framework I used to move from good, better, to best. I started by removing the mental barriers, the glass ceiling in my thinking, and self-imposed restrictions.

This work allowed me to look within and create the tools needed for fulfillment and for purpose to live the best version of myself daily.

My transition was focused on making mindful efforts to advance my inner wellbeing.

I'm sure many of you can relate to living by defined standards or something being insistent on defining your place in this world.

I'd lived much of my life like this, being focused on being "Good." I was "good" when things were going right. I pretended to be "good" through the downfalls and the pain associated with the losses. But subconsciously I was never "good" within myself. So early on in life, I developed a higher threshold for pain. This allowed me to have the appearance of being "good." My inner spirit was in constant contrast with my perpetual actions.

However, I've learned there is a way to make pain work in your favor by understanding the application of using the contrast between how bad it feels to hurt and how good it feels not to hurt. The contrast can motivate you to make a new choice that will enable you to endure wellbeing rather than ongoing hell. This practice of theory didn't come easy or without set back. Even today, I spend hours reflecting on the application of these tools and learning that every situation isn't going to go as planned. This allows me to handle the obstacles and practice continual grit through the roadblocks.

Within the world of competitive sports and training, we have a mantra, "No pain, and no gain." Most of us struggle and suffer a lot more than we need to and many of us could benefit from more kindness to self rather than pushing and fighting to endure the situations that rob us of joy.

Webster's New World Dictionary defined good as: enjoyable or satisfying; having the right qualities of high standard.

We must be clear about our personal interpretations of who defines the standards we live by and how the process makes us feel internally. Using the contrast tool helped me and hopefully it'll help you to transition from being unconscious to aware, and ultimately, over time, to self-aware.

We learn to blur or deny the signals from our inner core by simply telling ourselves we are good and continuing to ignore the hindering effects from distressing physical or emotional situations. Often this occurs below the level of our conscious awareness, where the pain is not acute, but builds gradually.

Our individual daily goal should reflect the actions of self-awareness and wellbeing. The journey of self-awareness takes us to a higher level of consciousness, allowing a complete transformation in our thoughts to ensure they align with our actions. This disarms any potential threats to our personal growth.

This transition calls for us to disallow others and their belief system to distract us from our calling. In your heart you know what feels good and what works, and this is your most reliable source. It is in trusting that inner source that will help us transcend from good to better.

Webster's New World Dictionary defines better as: more suitable, more desirable; being more than half; favorable, more profitable.

Many times, when I'm in thought, I turn to what seems to soothe my spirit at that moment. It could be journaling, reading, music, or just being still. I've learned the importance of defining the thought and accepting views that may differ from my own comprehension, which is also imperative to our growth.

This leads me to the definition of "better" and how it applies to that journey. The terminology is somewhat vague, as it doesn't refer to being complete. It speaks of being more favorable, or more than half. We should seek more from ourselves than just a more suitable outcome. In laxity terms . . . just being something you could settle for or live with is not satisfactory to me.

However, in a search for that greater sense of wellbeing, shouldn't we require more for ourselves? The term "mediocrity" is derived from the Latin connotations which are broken down to medio, which means "mid" and "ocrity," meaning mountain, compounded together refers to being "mid-mountain." It's not the highest point in our journey. It is a state of mind that removes mediocrity, favorable outcomes, and allows for us to be in the best possible space. It is my belief that we owe ourselves that much. By reaching to the depths of our core, and seeking wholeness, we're not just merely the more than half that it defines for us.

Imagine having an important surgical procedure scheduled, and during your pre-op consultation, your doctor stated, "I'm looking to get you the most favorable results." I think we'd all run for the nearest exit. So, why would we seek less for our inner wellbeing?

I've spoken openly with all of you about my poor choices and the cost of those mistakes. For many years of my life, I was good with the choices and accepted when things were favorable, but today those terms, those mind states, and those life positions no longer align with my personal expectations, goals or vision for my life.

I seek to do more than just survive in this world. I've implemented plans and goals that are realistic and will ensure that I thrive in my journey The road and paths taken have been the toughest terrain imaginable. I'm no longer focused on pitfalls, speed bumps or setbacks. The reward for me is the growth along the way.

Today, I understand my mistakes don't limit me, only fears can do that. Every day you wake up, you have a second chance to live that day as you envision for yourself. By making the most of all situations, you enliven your outcomes. If you seek to live wholeheartedly, you must stop accepting half measures. Thus, ensuring your pathway to the "best" viable net results.

Once again, there are no exact coordinates to the "best' version of us; that milestone is your interpersonal design. The road you choose shapes the experiences you encounter. Just be decisive with your plan of action, set realistic goals, and have patience in your process. The universe will do the rest. "Anywhere is paradise, it's up to you."

Best

Webster's New World Dictionary defines "best" as of the most excellent sort, surpassing all others.

We've spoken about the deconstruction phase and the transitions required in obtaining the mental accountability along your path. There is also a work of artistry to rendering that which is coming to life as well. Let's refer to it as construction and during this phase we understand construction is usually messy. You may have to turn the ground over, tear down existing structure, or pile materials all over the place. Construction projects are rarely neat and organized. They require some disorder and sprawl. Likewise, sometimes your life feels stable when you're in the good or better phase. And other times it's subject to demolition, construction or chaos; or all three. We are always in a state of becoming . . . this is an element of the human journey. Do not resist or begrudge the messy construction stage.

The vision of being the "best" version of us can be a magnificent reality. As you envision this path, the rendering takes flight. Behold a grand glorious version of where you are headed – far more beautiful and functional than the previous mindsets. Sometimes you cannot see the possibilities, and you have no idea where your life is moving.

Nothing happens in a vacuum; everything leads to something else. What appears to be a loss may be one event in a string of events that lead to something more rewarding than any single upsetting event?

CHAPTER ELEVEN

Dreams and Visions

"We affirm the court's long history of recognizing that one's past does not dictate one's future."

~ Washington Supreme Court Justice (Mary I. Yu)

As early as I can remember from my childhood, I was always a big dreamer. I spent time dreaming of the entire places I would go; all the things I would buy; even the mansion I would live in. Like most children, I had a seemingly large imagination, none of this seemed far-fetched. The fantasy of my dreams at 7 years of age made perfect sense to me. I couldn't imagine any other life for myself. There was no indication from my perceived reality, that we were impoverished, and we resided in a marginalized group of citizens, and to change my circumstances would require masterful calculation and years of hard work. Similar, to most children, I wanted it all right now.

Fast forwarding, that in the steps reality of those childhood dreams would be the disposition of my life as an adult. I learned the invaluable lesson of "Dreams vs. Visions."

We are all taught to dream and dream big. However, as we mature there's a more subsequent need to create a concise indicator for finding the path to our goals. We need to engage our intellect to concentrate on the visions for our lives.

In order to establish the outline for bringing our visions to fruition, we must search deep within ourselves. We need to define what that unique gift or talent is, and how to apply it. There is also a need to make sure your visions are self-fulfilling and not to impress anyone else.

So, now the question becomes how do I begin to clarify my visions? There are many solutions that we could look at to being clarification to your question. You may want to write down some fundamental ideals, then access what you've written and work from a process of elimination.

For me, it was expressing the ideals of how my four basic human needs are being met: physical, spiritual, and social or emotional. Does my vision represent a lifetime of balance of my personal, family, work, and community roles? Making sure that I'm inspired on the most essential levels is of foremost importance.

I started with a personal mission statement, and then I created a prosperity plan. These two essential components ensured I would have a well-grounded plan and foundation to build from. Many successful people believe in writing a mission statement. Yes! This matches the . . . same purpose as companies. Ensure your vision is in alignment with your needs of life or business. If you decide to use these tools as a guideline, make sure you write them down. Statistics have proven that roughly only about 5 percent of all people write down their goals. So, let's remain in the top of that class and ensure you have a clear, visible reflection of what you want to accomplish, and the steps needed to achieve the vision. By doing so, it also gives you a realistic point of reference that is multifarious at best.

The biggest challenges we face are our inability to think outside the box or our current level of comfort. Remember in order to achieve something you have never had; you must be willing to do something you have never done. Thus, requiring us to leave the box we sometimes place ourselves within. Secondly, we must begin with the end in mind, by beginning each day or task with a clear understanding of what we value as important, where we want to go, and how to get there. Every day, week, month, year, or longer period of time or task should begin with the end in mind. Otherwise, we may be setting ourselves up for failure.

I've had to realign the things that are of greatest value to me in my life. It has given me the clearest definition of vision I have as a man versus the dreams I had as a child. Now, I begin with the end in mind on all levels.

In closing, I will share my personal mission statement with you all. I truly hope it inspires you to live through your visions and seek each day to be the best version of yourself.

My personal mission statement:

- **I am an intelligent, innovative, warm-hearted person. The most important things in the world to me are my relationships with my family and friends, my spiritual connections, and my passion for my vision and work.**

- **I will constantly look for opportunities to learn and grow in my personal life. I dedicate myself to living in truth and purpose. I am determined to live by thriving and not just survival.**

- **I will find joy and laughter in all things daily, to make life more enjoyable and purposeful to myself and my loved ones.**

- **I will do my best to live a life of service to my family, work, in my spiritual community, and in all of the communities I strive to serve or assist.**

In the book "Principles" by Ray Dalio, he said "time is like a river that carries us forward to encounters with reality that requires us to make decisions. We can't stop our movement down this river and we can't avoid these encounters. We can only approach them in the best way possible."

~ Ray Dalio

CHAPTER TWELVE

Life Begins When You Say So

Resilience: The ability to recover rapidly from illness, change, or misfortune.

When I decided to share my testimony, struggles and journey with the rest of the world, I understood the risk of judgment, skepticism, and ridicule. However, it was more important for me to use my story to empower other individuals who may be experiencing similar challenges in their lives. I aspire to introduce the concepts and tools I use in my daily decision-making process to find freedom and inner peace. By sharing and supporting others, we often gain more within ourselves. Giving in many ways is more fulfilling than receiving.

The concepts I practice are the ladder that pulls me up from the rudiments of my past choices in life. They are merely perspectives and are not intended to be the blueprint for anyone's choices or actions. Rather, they are a shift in the ideology of our thought patterns.

The concept of "life begins when you say so," is and forever will be definitive for me. Time is the most precious gift we are awarded in our lifetime. I have certainly wasted more than my share of this gracious gift we are all afforded. This is my personal acknowledgment and testament to my commitment to change.

There are approximately 86,400 seconds in any given day. This includes your sleep time. From the moment you awaken, the clock is ticking and running. Yesterday doesn't really matter, and tomorrow isn't present yet. So, every moment should be directed towards thriving in your current space daily.

Often, we await the right opportunity, persons, jobs, financial stability, and most importantly wellbeing to present them. Then we can begin to live, love, earn, or even relax. However, life just doesn't work that way; it is a continual process. The mere suggestion of waiting for the right time places your liberty in a state of stagnation.

Living as we know it is more than just the celebratory period; it's the sum of all. Each day we must make the most of the opportunities that each sacred moment offers.

I had to learn some really enlightening lessons the hard way. I took for granted the value of liberty and choice. I had to stretch myself. By stretching myself, I was able to challenge myself, my views, and subsequently things began to be different. It's always important to get outside of your comfort zone; then and only then can you expand your consciousness. In order to change your life, you have to change the way you think.

I had spent a vast majority of my adulthood trying to create a lifestyle of comfort. When, in all actuality, I was enabling my vitality. This was in total contrast to the objective I desired.

So, today a major goal for me in my personal development is to learn and apply all this knowledge towards attaining effectiveness, understanding, and emotional wellbeing while sharing the knowledge with other individuals.

This is the purpose I have found for my life. Each day I awake, the gift of a new day is present, and I'm living my life to the fullest of my capabilities. I don't spend a moment complaining. I may be incarcerated currently, but my life is headed the direction of my choices daily. There's no moment when you will arrive. Spend each moment learning, creating, and giving back. "Life begins when you say so."

CHAPTER THIRTEEN

The Transformation Process

"What you think becomes what you believe, what you believe determines how you behave. How you behave determines what you experience. Anonymous

Wow! This concept became the most enlightening part of my journey thus far. In the earlier chapters, I expressed my dissension throughout my adolescence. I discussed my shortcomings during my teenage to young adult stages. In particular, this irrationality led to my faulty belief system as an adult; nothing destroys the human psyche more than low self-esteem.

For instance, I grew up poor, which led me to the inadequacy I sometimes felt as a child. The desolation associated to my family's economic position caused me shame daily. Consequently, I created the falsehood that would create great complexity many years later in my life.

As a result, my personal transformation process would begin to unfold. In Chapter Two, I shared the consequences associated with my actions; namely having to finally examine my thought process. In particular, I processed the self-destructive behaviors of going to prison, and the collateral damage to my family, who would suffer gravely because of my selfish actions.

Therefore, in this process, I needed to not only re-examine my priorities, but I had to establish and implement a sincere commitment to change.

Thus, my process really began to evolve. I started by making amends to my family and people whom I felt I had let down.

Furthermore, I accepted responsibility for my conduct as well as my shortcomings. Also, I had to practice forgiveness daily. Forgiveness to myself and forgiveness to others who I felt had wronged me. Despite the situation or challenges, I was all-in with a heightened sense of determination. For the first time in my life, I sat down and actually created a plan for my life. Specifically, I set goals for myself, both short-term and long-term. Moreover, I examined my capacity to fulfill the vision I had for my life. I always had thoughts and ideals, but I lacked the direction or real sense of purpose concerning my life. Setting goals gave me something to strive for. However, defining my purpose gave me something greater than myself to exist for.

Besides, finding something greater than myself to exist for, I needed to find a way to be of service to others, even in my current situation. I practiced ways to show empathy to others who were also going through dark periods in their lives. I worked to consistently practice humility in my daily actions, because it's important to release all sense of entitlement. I clearly understand that dynamic, because I felt the world owed me something greater than what I experienced as a child growing up impoverished. As a result, that misguided belief system would directly correlate to me being incarcerated for several terms of imprisonment. Like I stated earlier, I never really had a knowing problem. I always felt as though I knew what I wanted to do. I lacked the wherewithal to put the needed work in to achieve the desired outcomes.

I had experienced some semblance of tangible achievement, or social recognition. Yet, I erroneously accepted that as a victory in my personal life when nothing could have been further from the truth.

The truth is, our real private victories are established when we enrich the lives of those around us. This is the primary motivation in my personal journey today.

The process of transformation is not a destination, rather a series of intricate steps we must take daily, or hourly if need be. I would be the first to say long ago that people don't change. However, nothing about that statement bears truth. We are all capable of change. Humans evolve for the greater good or stagnation about every five years. Your level of growth is directly related to the level of work and dedication you put forth along your journey to becoming better. Each day we are all given the same gift of a new day, and with that precious gift we can choose to create opportunities. These opportunities translate into our inner personal achievements.

Today, I understand you must commit to your personal level of change. Namely, what you envision for yourself. It is my belief that, if you can envision it, comprehend your capacity for something greater; then your transformation process awaits you remember change is possible!

CHAPTER FOURTEEN

Time, the Real Gift

"We see the world not as it is, but as we are."

Source unknown

Often, we judge our days by what we get done or achieve. But true beauty are the moments of awakening, joy, or insight you experience. Your activities are simply a template of your journey. If, in the midst of busyness, you find and absorb moments that move you, your day is successful. If you get a lot done, but do not feel closer to yourself or life, the day did not yield real fruit.

Most of us spend our days shuffling along from task to task; we may even have that infamous "to do list." Yet, seemingly, we're never fulfilled within ourselves with the requirements and demands of our time. We continue this pattern day in and out only placing more emptiness in our lives.

This vital gift that I wasted would ultimately be the inspiration of this chapter. We are all blessed with 86,400 moments a day. The outcome of our daily life will be a mirror of what we did with the gift of today.

I look at photos of my loved ones during special moments and events, and I'm reminded of the lapse in my use of this gift. Time lost cannot be restored. Time cannot be fast-forwarded; all we have is the gift of today. Yesterday is no longer of importance; our focus must remind us of the blessings of today.

Life is meaningful not for the seconds that tick by, but for the moments that fill them. There are a few attributes of the gift of time that we take for granted daily.

I chose so early on how my gift would be spent, and I live with that daily. Nonetheless, for those of you who are blessed with the gift each new day brings, I encourage you to use your time wisely. Live unselfishly, live to create joy in your life and the lives of others daily. Remember, the universe hasn't promised tomorrow; make the most of the real gift of time.

> *"The more clearly you see, the*
> *better the world becomes and the*
> *more I improve my position to*
> *create effective change."*
> unknown.

CHAPTER FIFTEEN

Friends, Social Connections

"A mirror reflects a man's face, but what he is really like is shown by the kinds of friends he chooses." Unknown

A message to the youth:

The simple, but true fact of life is, you become like those who you closely associate with whether for the good or bad.

I've learned a lot of tough lessons, but none hit home more than this reflection I'm going to share with you. There are few great examples in life than those we grow from. It does not matter how many attempts you have to make, but it is more important that you never give up.

Although, we are solely responsible for our choices and our actions. Social influences attribute to the majority of the negative decisions we make as young adults and in some cases as grown adults.

The importance of friends and social connections is a vital component to our wellbeing. In fact, it is highly imperative that we choose our relationships wisely. For some adolescents, these years are the most challenging, trying to fit in or find acceptance within your group of peers, and for some the bonds established become greater than parental bonds or bonds with a sibling. As a result, the pressure to fit in, or be popular, has caused an increasingly high level of depression and suicide amongst the youth.

Growing up an only child, I faced a multitude of challenges. I got caught up in a troublesome lifestyle so early on. In earlier chapters, I shared my journey to becoming greater than my worst mistakes. Specifically, the particulars that led me down that path. My intentions are never to glamorize the street life. However, I recognize the need for the youth to understand the realities of how poor choices can impact your entire life. I want to share the facts of how a simple poor choice changes the trajectory of your future; the potential loss of liberty, free will, and in some dire situations, life. I want to help shape the narrative, that it is better to be alone, than to be in the wrong company. "If you want to be successful, it is crucial that you remove the losers from your life."

So, early on I gravitated towards surroundings that were detrimental to my growth; it was mostly out of pure boredom. This led to delinquency and lack of positive social adaptation. I was hanging with a crowd that expected nothing from me and reinforced my negative actions. When you're doing the wrong things in life, you surround yourself with people who also behave in the same capacity. The problem with this behavior is that it's self-destructive, and usually leads to a life of incarceration, drug addiction, and mortality.

Surrounding ourselves with people who don't care about themselves, or others, will ultimately cost you more than the foreseeable present. It may appear to be cool, being around those whom you feel you can relate to or who don't appear to judge you. On the contrary, I assure you it's only fake acceptance, and it's only going to keep you trapped in a cycle of decay.

Think of it this way, it's impossible for someone who loves you and cares about you to sit back, and watch you destroy yourself or your life. The one decision you make in just a minute of time could destroy your future.

I know firsthand what it's like to feel lost or just want to escape. Nevertheless, the path that behavior leads to is a price too grave to pay for being lost or misunderstood.

I think of those choices I made so early on and there are days I wish that I could speak to that young man, just as I'm sharing with you all now. I would share this vital information:

- Soak up the wisdom around you.
- Make time to dream big dreams and surround yourself with people who believe in them.
- Be ready to lay your own foundation, don't allow yourself to be pigeonholed. Create the goals that allow you an opportunity to pivot and never be backed into a corner. Move in positive directions.
- Seize your moments – make your education the single most important investment you make.
- Keep your real friends close.
- Make your parents proud.
- Honor the place you come from – and community you reside in.
- Do the work – then enjoy the ride.

I'm encouraging you to find a group of peers or friends who are positive, have goals, and want to make something of their lives.

There may be times when your situation seems hopeless, and you may feel as though you have no support; some of you may feel unloved. Or your family maybe broken up by an incarcerated parent, or by drug addiction or alcohol abuse. Regardless, if you can make a choice to do something positive each day, your life can and will change for the better.

It may not happen overnight, but it will happen. You first have to want to make things better for yourself. Take responsibility for your life and your actions. Start each day off doing something that will change your current situation. It doesn't have to be anything major; start where you are now (read, exercise, find laughter, talk with someone). Get far away from any negative people or situations.

Most importantly, if you are experimenting with drugs or alcohol, "STOP," and seek help. You have your whole life ahead of you, even though you can't see what that looks like right now. You are ten times greater than anything that has happened to you.

In conclusion, begin by finding someone you feel safe enough to confide in. Then, allow them to listen and help you find the resources to assist you. Believe me, there are many people out there who do care and want to help you. If there's anything that you care about, enjoy doing, or are curious to learn, share those things and allow the process to work. Be patient; change takes time. Lastly, remember if you associate with wolves, you will learn how to howl, but if you associate with eagles, you will learn to soar to great heights. This is my purpose in my life, to give back and help someone else avoid the pitfalls of poor choices. Don't follow anyone who is not going anywhere. Be blessed, your destiny awaits you!

CHAPTER SIXTEEN

Financial Literacy

A message to the African American Community:

Experts say people often must make difficult decisions to sustain themselves. "It's not a question of being smart or being thoughtful or planning for the future. You are forced to make a series of bad decisions when life doesn't work with wages that low."

~ USA Today on Minimum Wage.

There's an ever-urgent need for our communities to wake up and take notice of the financial impoverishment within the African American Community in the United States.

We must acknowledge the problems, seek resolution, and gain knowledge concerning the financial mind state that plagues our culture today. No longer can we sit idle complaining of inequality. We must begin by looking at the behaviors that leave us last economically

We, as African Americans, live in the wealthiest country in the universe. Unfortunately, 98 percent of our populated culture are too busy with the day-to-day task of trying to earn a living to ever make any real progress toward their vision of financial independence. Most of us work hard all of our lives yet fail to develop the habit of spending less than we earn. Sadly, even in a country known for its level of opportunity, most men and women of color will probably never achieve a lifestyle of financial freedom.

In the United States, poverty is defined for African Americans as a family of four earning below $25,094 a year, according to the US Census Bureau and the US Department of Commerce. And yet, tragically, many hardworking deserving people of color spend their entire lives with their shoulder to the wheel only to end up financial failures in a country where opportunity is unlimited.

One of the largest problems within our community is we buy and spend, and many times commit our hard-earned dollars to everyone else, never keeping any for ourselves. Unfortunately, creating a greater gap in the generational poverty cycle. In essence, we give away all our economic power. But, in order to fully grasp the financial ability within our communities, we must first be able to see our actual authority.

African Americans account for nearly a quarter of a trillion dollars a year in consumer spending. That, in itself, is nearly incomprehensible, if we didn't have access to the data on consumer spending.

Ask yourself how can a family of four living below poverty level truly succeed? How can the population of less than 36 percent account for so much financial wastefulness? When the medium income for a single African American male is merely $29,962 a year, and the medium income for a single African American female is $23,499 a year, according to the 2017 Economic Analysis by US Census Bureau, US Department of Commerce. More staggering data exists to make you take notice of the financial ruins we are in within our communities. While you may find this statistical data hard to fathom, it is a current reality for too many African Americans who are struggling to provide the essentials for their families, such as food and shelter.

Nearly 30.7 percent of African American female households with no male present are below poverty. Compared to 23.9 percent of single white females with no males' present (according to the US Census data poverty by race 2017).

A real conversation is needed in our households, in our churches, or wherever we gather in masses to bring this discussion to the forefront. There seems to be a real disconnect within our culture on our spending habits.

We're last in the categories needed to establish wealth such as: home ownership, investments, retirement planning, estate planning, and most importantly tuition planning for our children. Black owned businesses have decreased compared to our ancestors. Granted, we have made many vast improvements. However, we are still dead last in the race for financial freedom.

Furthermore, so many of us lack knowledge of some of the financial greats who were not athletes or entertainers. They were hardworking people like many of us who had the determination and grit to sustain through all adversity they faced daily. Inhumane laws, segregation, and racism were just as prevalent then as the forms that exist today. Fortunately, they didn't wait for the system or the government to which they battled for human rights to fix their problems. The list of greats is astonishing. They didn't have the platform that many have today, yet they inspired many. I'm speaking of Ed Gardner and Soft Sheen, Madame C.J. Walker, Surgeon General Joycelyn Elders, author Samuel Smiles, Percy Sutton, John H. Johnson, Wilma Rudolph (world sprinter), Arthur G. Gaston, an ex-steel mill worker who was a . . . self-made millionaire/entrepreneur. He created a simple formula that he lived by. He was a man of skill and mindset. He fought hard for others and sought to serve. He settled upon a chosen profession and was a firm believer in "continued personal development." He had an analogy that each of us, whether we realize it or not, has the same opportunity to employ the qualities needed to succeed. He also understood that only a few individuals knew how to properly use their earnings. "We can earn it, hoard it, spend it, save it, waste it, or worship it. But to deal with it wisely, as a means to an end, is an education worth its weight in gold." He shared this simple formula to creating financial independence with us:

- Save a portion of all you earn. Delay gratification, spend less, save more, pay yourself first. To compound interest is a money-making tool so use it.
- Establish a reputation at a bank or save at a reputable institution.
- Don't lose money. A man or woman who can't afford to lose money has no business gambling.
- Never borrow anything you can't pay back.
- Specialize, find a need and fill it. Successful businesses are built on the needs of others.

- Once you launch your business, keep good books and hire the best people you can find.

These great minds, works of our ancestors, demonstrate the ability of our culture.

So much of our wellness work is inner connected. This insight on financial literacy is just another small, intricate piece of a larger puzzle helping us create dialogue and understanding from perspectives outside of our own.

I had many discussions with various people who share different views on reparations and social equality. Respectfully, I cannot waiver on my opinion and position concerning the need to understand where we are in this economic cycle. I dispel the belief that we need government assistance. You can't solve real problems by throwing money at the issues. If you give the poor money, that will simply stop them from being broke for about a week. If we as African Americans are still poor in our minds, then we will continue the dreaded cycle of poverty.

Every poor person in our communities has to learn how to climb that ladder out of poverty. However, each of us has a responsibility to mentor, create internships, businesses, and jobs within our community. It is my belief that this is the only way to fix generational poverty that exists in this country today.

In conclusion, how can people who contribute so much end up dead last on the financial totem pole? We must become wealth conscious. Prosperity, wealth, and abundance are normal, a way of life. They are an active way of thinking and living within the spiritual and mental laws of abundance and supply. It is only empty heads that constantly spend with no concern for their legacy. I wish health and prosperity for us as a culture and our communities. It starts with gaining financial literacy.

CHAPTER SEVENTEEN

Spiritual Awareness

"Never let your senses of morals keep you from doing what is right."

People often ask me my religious preference or affiliation. For a long time, I pondered the answer. Growing up, I would sometimes attend a Baptist church, so my beliefs were those associated with the Baptist teachings. Later, in my pre-teens, I was introduced to the Nation of Islam. I was immediately drawn to its disciplines for African American men. By the same token, I realized how implausible it would be for me to live up to those expectations. Subsequently, in my adult years, my attendance would dwindle from all doctrines. As a result, this left me with a spiritual void.

As time progressed, I began to question the teachings from my earlier experiences with the different genres of religious teachings. I often judge the actions of clergymen and their personal transgressions. Those actions interfered with my personal spiritual relationship with a higher power. I wondered, "Is there truly a God?" And, if such a Being existed; how could there be so much hardship in this world? There couldn't be this omnipresent force that allows so much suffering, murder, and loss of innocent life. It became easier to blame this force for my choices and actions. I projected the consequences of my actions on His love and mercy in my life. It wasn't before long I would only seek this presence during hardships in my life, feeling each attempt as a fail to gain the sought-after assistance through my dilemmas.

Then, something really began to shift in my thinking. As I accepted responsibility for my actions, and sought to gain greater understanding, I found what I define as "spiritual awareness." During my quest for knowledge, this concept became the blueprint for my enlightenment. I discovered that religion is infinite, and its depth is vast. The arguments on theology are far too complex for a man or woman to fully interpret, leaving us with an ambiguous understanding at best.

However, what is more important than denomination or declaration of faith is for us as human beings to have spiritual consciousness. This spiritual consciousness . . . understands that there is a creator of all life, and we must have a connection to this higher power. This allows us to find purpose in something greater than self.

In developing this awareness, you could picture two overlapping circles. One circle represents religion and the other circle represents spirituality. There is a portion of religion that is spiritual and a portion of spirituality that is religious. You can be spiritual without being religious, and you can be religious without being spiritual. Our higher power does not dwell more intensely in one belief over the other.

Our spiritual consciousness requires us to establish a connection that helps us evolve as humans. A clearer understanding of that connection allows us to live closer to that belief. Thus, ensuring we all make greater contributions to the world around us.

In Buddhism, the Dalai Lama declared, "His religion is Kindness." This is the passage to your spiritual awareness.

Specifically, I focus on my truths and on my heart being in alignment. I focus on my inner sense and having faith in that inner knowing. Therefore, I am right with my higher power, because I am right with myself.

In conclusion, the future may be unknowable, but I am empowered and emboldened knowing I can help others through my actions. I am blessed with a powerful awareness that my spiritual vision can help direct my life, as I open up to the activity of God in me. My thoughts and words are affirmation for my vision of my life. The testimony I share propels me toward the realization of my goals. I keep my mind open to all possibilities through my spiritual awareness. I pray that all who seek shall truly find understanding and peace. I'm a firm believer in "we get what we expect." Choose your path to your spiritual awareness.

CHAPTER EIGHTEEN

Inspiration

"If you view all the things that happen to you, both good and bad, as opportunities, then you operate out of a higher level of consciousness" Les Brown

There were times in my life where things were moving so fast, I could barely keep up. Reflecting on those moments during my time in 'the life,' time seemed to go by so quickly. The days rolled into nights, and the nights turned into weeks. I couldn't find the simplicity of enjoying the sunshine on a summer day or a perfect reflection of a rainbow. It always seemed as though my mind was in a hundred different places all at once. I guess for the most part, I have been like that throughout most of my life, or as early as I can remember.

I attest to most of my inspiring moments transpiring in my darkest hours. Some of the most painful lessons would become my greatest strengths and defining approach to my desire for change. But I would make many other mistakes before I fully committed to changing my thinking.

Most of my life goals were all associated with making money. While making money was good, my life lacked having an emotional connection to my career and meaningful healthy relationships. To me, meaningful work meant doing something I could earn lots of money doing. So, I became engrossed in my definition of success. This ultimately led to my demise. I wasted so many years of my life. Upon this journey, I discovered a quote from Emerson, which became the fuel to my inspiration. "We become what we think about all day long." I concentrated on those words and repeated the mantra to the man in the stainless-steel reflection. "We become what we think about all day long." I thought about those words intently and gazed into my miserable reality.

I stared at the reflection and noticed I was getting old. My teens had raced by at warp speed. I noticed lines on my face that I hadn't noticed before. I was growing older before my very eyes. How had I wasted so much of my life? How had I allowed things to get so out of control? Was it too late to do anything about it? After all, I wouldn't see the streets again until I as nearly 60 years old. I considered Emerson's words once more. Again, I wondered. Was there more to life? What would I need to do to find out? I questioned if I was even remotely capable of altering the course of my seemingly forged destiny?

Was it possible to become something different by thinking something different? Despite seemingly insurmountable odds, I decided to find out. Thus, my inspiration for change was formulated and I began to seek to understand rather than to be understood. I began to practice empathy, placing the people that I considered most important first for once in my whole existence. By practicing these simple, but yet complex steps, my mind began to see other possibilities that were once closed to me because of my thinking. I grew to understand that having meaningful relationships would require active participation in nurturing those people I cared for deeply, and who cared for me.

I began to see how senseless it was to have achieving wealth as the main priority in my life. The mere fact that money has no intrinsic value spoke in volumes to my misguided belief system. I began to seek knowledge and to learn at every given opportunity. I found inspiration in wisdom and became hungry for more.

As I stated earlier, inspiration can come at any moment in your life. It can become . . . life altering or empowering. Both ways, it's a divine gift from the universe and it's completely free. Our only fee is to look beyond our situations by practicing being a blessing in someone else's life or circumstance. This form of empathy gives us purpose in our lives whether we can see it or not. This allows us as humans to live through love and not just material attainments. We begin to remove the "I" and find understanding for others. We should consider what someone else may be experiencing, feeling or needing. And, for that we can enhance this universe we live in just that much more.

It's through the process of discovery that we will be able to share our individual gifts and talents with the world around us. So, just as my journey has inspired me to share my testimonies, I hope that you are inspired as you continue on your pathway of enlightenment. It also serves to remind me of my personal responsibility to share information to enrich the lives of others. I celebrate and learn from people who see the wonder in life. They have become my teachers of achieving peace and balance during all phases of my journey.

CHAPTER NINETEEN

Creating and Defining your Success

"Whatever you expect, with confidence becomes your own self-fulfilling prophecy."

~

G rowing up, ultimately, I was taught early on not to expect too much from life. There was an unspoken rule that in order for me to be something I had to get a good job and earn a decent living to help provide for myself and my future family. The difficulty begins when we allow our destiny to be defined by others (peers, idols, siblings, and even potential spouses). Encouragement is always a welcomed tool, but the dreams and visions should be yours. I don't recall anyone saying to me that you can grow up to own your own business, or one day you may create something the world needs. I recall some of the talks with my foster mother; she was always encouraging and talked about success quite often. But she never really revealed the steps I needed to take to create the success I visualized others achieve.

For many of us, we've learned to be successful by societal terms, and how it is derived through hard work, good strategies, and determination. There are many adequate terms to satisfy the scholars who give recognition to those who achieve or perform at higher levels.

However, for most of us, our work is inner-personal and reflective to its application in our day-to-day journey. Understanding this concept helps those of us who may feel unsuccessful or non-productive.

Defining what success really means to us gives us consistent frameworks to shape our ideology and worry less about external classifications.

In my personal experiences these findings gave me the perspective to create, improve, and empower the growth mindset I needed to achieve realistic goals and also my personal wellbeing.

By asking yourself honest questions, you can gain the insight needed to create a growth mind state, thus, allowing you to eliminate negative beliefs which can ultimately disrupt your chances for success.

You first want to start by choosing questions that help you establish your outlook on success and being successful.

These questions will . . . help to identify the key factors that prohibit you from unlocking your fullest potential. Here are some sample questions you could use as your template: Is your success defined by external factors? Such as: jobs, relationships, status, financial, or material accomplishments? Do you feel more successful when acknowledged for an accomplishment? Are good work evaluations, job performance, or promotion your defining moment? Do you associate non-productivity with being unsuccessful and, if so, why?

For example, would a wife who stays home to provide for her children while the spouse works be defined as unsuccessful? Likely not; there are many people in today's society who serve in roles that play an intricate part in the functionality of our everyday world who are just as successful as any CEO.

The nanny who cares for your children, the maid who cleans your home, or the server who brings you coffee during your business meetings all of these people are successful regardless of title or status. That's why it is vital that we define our success.

What's important to some may be deemed less important to others. However, our success is and forever will be defined solely by us. It is the contributions, service or input we extend to make not only our lives richer, but rather, helping to enrich the lives of others that give real definition to the term success.

It starts with aligning our core values with our goals. Then we assess the actions and behaviors we display to achieve the desired outcome. Gaining a definitive understanding provides an opportunity to operate in a capacity of a mind state that ensures inner-personal growth. This enables the success we desire to be achievable on any and all levels

We started with the question "what defines your success?" Now, let's look at some of the actions from a growth mind state to help achieve our vision of success. Be mindful that our thoughts drive our actions, so the actions must be appropriate for our goals to be attainable.

The actions must also be associated with proper boundaries, rather than just being deeds. This means they are solely committed to our growth at every stage of development. We use boundaries to offset setbacks we face daily. We should never allow ourselves to fall into insecurities or defensiveness, a response that could inhibit our growth.

Growth-minded actions support our goals and lead to inner-personal success. Here are some examples:

- **Inner calm and contentment**
- **Sense of openness**
- **Feeling of safety**
- **Purposefulness, dedication**
- **Self-confidence**
- **Sense of worth**
- **Engagement, commitment**

No matter the obstacle, setbacks, challenges, or hardships, we must work daily to display actions associated through the process of constant thought. This leads to our growth and wellbeing. We must use these tools as the cornerstone, to create and define our success. As a result, affirming our journey toward success is an inner-personal achievement, and can only be measured by our wellbeing, not societal standards.

If we are to improve the results in our lives, we must begin by upgrading our beliefs and expectations and by deepening our recognition of our self-worth. We merit kindness, respect, enjoyable surroundings, financial rewards, and success by our definition. If we expect so people who surround us and situations that affect us will reflect our beliefs.

In conclusion, I once read "the script of our life is etched in our minds, and the people we encounter are actors in the movie of our lives we have written." Regardless of what scenes that have played out in our lives, we have the ability, with the blessings of each new day, to rewrite the story. Search your mind for the good you expect to find, and it will happen. No matter the circumstances, "you are ten times greater than the worst thing that has happened to you." You must create and define your success.

CHAPTER TWENTY

A Win-Win Formula

"The ultimate measure of a man is not where in moments of comfort and convenience, but where he stands at times of challenge and controversy." God's Instruction for Men

Y ou cannot define success by how little you lose. The purpose of life is not to minimize your losses, but to maximize your gains. If you have lost a lot, psychologically, you may become so accustomed to losing that winning seems like a fantasy. For me, that success was driven by money and the illusion of having success was based on wealth.

When I speak of a "Win-Win Formula," I'm not simply referring to attaining money or having finances. However, I am referencing the exponential inner-personal rewards: joy, love, societal connections, creativity, and success as you define it. If your life is consumed with responding to emergencies, putting out fires, and damage control, consider what it would take for you to feel as though you are thriving rather than just surviving. Therefore, with that vision in mind, make choices from a sense of expansion instead of settling. That's how we're going to create a win-win formula.

We sometimes find ourselves stuck in a rut of mediocrity and we become stagnant, not because of who we are (our potential), but because of how we are (our behavior). Looking back on my false ideology of success, today I see how my behaviors and my fixed mindset were true obstacles.

I had no real core values that weren't associated with achieving fortune. Thus, my belief that money would and could cure all my problems. In fact, I truly believed success was defined by how little I lost. Boy was I sadly mistaken.

Subsequently, I believe the world can be divided into three kinds of people, based on the different ways they view the difficulties of life.

The first group of people feel like "it's over" before it begins. They see all the bad things that could happen to them or their dreams or plans so they attempt very little. They are convinced that anything they try will have a bad outcome and will never work. So, they refuse to get out of their comfort zone and therefore never become who they are meant to be.

The second group of people experienced such a terrible failure at some point that they came to believe "it's over." These individuals are not like the first group of people who never tried. They did try, but when they failed, they assumed the dismal outcome was the message about themselves, their dreams, and sometimes, if the failure was large enough itself, they let the failure tell them, "Forget it, you will never achieve." So, they came to believe that "it's over when it's over." Like the first group, they never become who they were meant to be. A particular failure stopped them from ever trying again.

The third group of people believe It's never over. They discover that if you have a few essential ingredients from which new life emerges, a failure or a death of any dream is never the end, but only the first step of a new beginning. Further, they allow their painful experiences to become a crucible within themselves. They do become who they were meant to be. They are reinvented through failure itself.

Society seldom hears of failures of high achievers, perhaps because it wants to think of these men and woman in terms of success, not failure. On the other hand, many accomplished performers or achievers often avoid talking about or dwelling on their setbacks. Sometimes, their setbacks are too painful to reflect upon. Still, occasionally, some will expand upon their failures long enough for others to learn a practical lesson from their experiences. This is my hope for you, the reader. Specifically, understanding that we can create a life for ourselves regardless of situation or physical circumstances. There is often very little mentioned of the obstacles many have faced in their attempt to create their "Win-Win Formula." The clear-cut assessment of many individuals who are successful anchors around setbacks and rejection. Achievement owes its growth to the striving of the will, the ability to overcome fear, and the ever-present danger of failure. Make no mistake about it, victories that come easy are cheap. And he or she who has never failed, has never really succeeded.

If we are to create a true and meaningful "win-win formula," we must first objectify our inner-personal goals. Identify the purpose of completing the objectives we seek. Ensuring, we are seeking fulfillment that is intrinsic, and we begin with the end in mind.

In conclusion, once we establish the purpose of our goals or objectives, we then can see a route or path to lead us to our milestone. Also, we must distinguish the roles we will play, as well as who will support us in our roles. For instance, one of my goals consists of closer family connections. The person who may assist me could be my spouse or children. By strengthening our family connections, we gain clarity and have someone to help us be accountable.

The other elements to your "Win-Win Formula," is being able to identify weaknesses in your vision or goals. This allows you to see any potential setbacks and ensures you have the fortitude to endure.

Finally, we can use these tools as a fundamental resource. The challenges will remain, but our mindset will be geared toward growth and achieving our goals against all odds. Remember along the way, the "Win-Win Formula" is comprised of your perception and attitude. The journey is all about growth - never the destination.

"Life begins at the end of your comfort zone."

~ unknown

Epilogue

Writer's Note

"It is not what you have lost, but what you have left."
Chucky Mullins

Justice Thurgood Marshall stated, "when the prison gates slam behind an inmate, he does not lose his human quality; his mind does not become closed to ideas; his intellect does not cease to feed on a free and open interchange of opinions; his yearning for self-respect does not end; nor his quest for self-realization concluded. If anything, the needs for identity and self-respect are more compelling in the dehumanizing prison environment."

Crucial to that need for self-improvement is the ability to read and study, to thereby learn new ideals and ways of thinking and thus behaving.

I have shared the concepts and tools I use daily to help anyone who may be in a dark space mentally or emotionally. We have looked at the impact of poor choices and found inspiration from loss and grief. We have discussed the importance of creating your success and facing your fears. We discovered the real gift of time as well as created a "Win-Win Formula" for our continued growth and wellbeing.

This book was created as a testimony:

- To the goodness of the universal process of life.
- Using each milestone in our everyday journey to evolve and gain a greater consciousness of self.
- To ensure we are doing the work daily to become more than our experiences.
- Allowing us to reach deep within ourselves and create the purpose in our lives, bringing inner-peace and fulfillment along our path.
- Defining the sum of our destiny "Against All Odds."

I leave you as I come in peace!

"I am your constant companion.

I am your greatest helper or

heaviest burden. I will push you

onward or drag you down to failure.

I am completely at your command. Half

the things you do, you might just as well

turn over to me and I will be able to

do them quickly and correctly. I am easily

managed – you must be firm with me.

Show me exactly how you want something done

and after a few lessons I will do it auto-

matically. I am the servant of all great

men; and alas, of all failures, as well.

Those who are great, I have made great.

Those who are failures, I have made failures.

I am not a machine, though I work with

all precision of a machine plus the intelli-

gence of a man. You may run me for

profit or run me for ruin – it

makes no difference to me. Take me,

train me, be firm with me, and I

will place the world at your feet. Be

easy with me and I will destroy

you. Who am I? I am habit! ~ Anonymous

Acknowledgments

They say when you expose your gifts or talents to the world, you open yourself up to envy and hate. Do you anyway!

It has been a journey! To the queens in my life: my mother, daughters, sisters, and nieces who give me inspiration to protect, and be the best version of myself every day.

To my sons – I love you and support each of you through your journeys to greatness. I learn from you, young men, daily.

To my brothers from other mothers: Reggie, Eddie, James, Alonzo, Gershaun and Lance. The realest dudes – love y'all. "Blood makes you related, but loyalty makes you family."

To my nephews: Special shout out to my rock, Rasheed, we did it man! To "Magic" be blessed wherever you are in this world thank you for being you. Love to you all.

An extended thanks to my friend and go to man, Mark Blankespoor and my brother Troy Brown.

A1SNCEDAY . . . Never Fold!

Contact us: DeVordJAllen@gmail.com

Coming Soon!

Risen from the Ashes

Life After the Game

A

Memoir

By

De'Vord J. Allen

Prologue

This memoir was written following my release from federal prison. The accounts are real and noted for factual purposes.

It is my sincerest intention to capture the mind of the reader, allowing an intimate inquest into my journey of becoming more than my experiences. I'll be sharing the pathways I've used daily and the struggles and obstacles I face attempting to live in my purpose.

In "Against All Odds," I spoke about creating goals, defining your success, and building a winning formula. "Risen from the Ashes" takes us to the doorstep of when preparation and opportunity meet. I've awaited the day my life would be taken off pause and begin to play as I design what the Most High Intended. "Through Him who strengthens me all things become possible." Philippians 4:13.

Looking back, the underground world had become a trend throughout the course of my younger years. I'd often convinced myself that I was doing what I had to do regardless of the consequences or collateral damage. In that culture, I lived by any means necessary with the misconception that the means justified the end.

Maybe it was a coping mechanism, going back to something I'd found success in when I wasn't experiencing it elsewhere. Whatever it was, it was a habit that went on in my life for much too long, longer than you'd expect or think considering I knew firsthand the consequences associated with those actions. But, like most young people, I was searching for instant gratification without the hard work associated with achieving a desired and favorable outcome.

Unlike so many guys in prison, I was getting another chance. My last chance. I couldn't drop the ball again. I needed to do more than pray, I needed to make better decisions. There was something brewing deep inside, questions that only I could answer. "How long can I keep going to prison? How long before everyone I truly love would give up on me because of my actions?"

I'd had 16 years to think about the relationships that mattered the most. Time to think . . . about the mistakes I can't afford to make again. Time to think about my strengths my shortcomings, and my limits. Time to think about the way I've got to respond when times get tough again because tough times are a part of life. Knowing it's how you bounce back from those moments that define who you are.

I would have to decide. Which direction would it be? Left or Right? I needed to be firm . . . in that decision, realizing at all times that it will not happen overnight.

To start a new chapter, you've got to turn the page on the last one. You can't keep looking back or you may trip forward.

Long ago, I thought I was a product of my environment. However, nothing could be further from the truth; I was a product of bad choices.

Incarceration can be a catalyst to produce individuals that emerge with a newfound moral compass. I am privileged to have experienced, as well as witnessed, that growth and development throughout my incarceration.

Prison is a place that was referred to as being the closest to death as one could get. Maybe it's the flashing white light many have spoken about before the final call. Or it could be that single moment the heart stops before resuscitation; where the defibrillator electronically shocks your heart to beat again. Whatever the defining moment, prison was like standing on a banana peel with one foot falling backwards into the shallow pit of demise, and the final chorus of life.

Somewhere amid this madness, there was something unbending in my will to overcome. I can't call it an epiphany, or some life altering moment. However, I will say at that exact moment my mind, heart, and spirit rose. The eternal rungs propelled me from the ashes of self-destruction. I wanted to change, I needed to change, and I sought a master plan for my life. Something greater than I'd known or ever experienced.

"If you want to achieve something you've never had, you must be willing to do something you've never done."

~

Anonymous

"Risen from the Ashes" is the testament to my journey.

"Against All Odds"

DeVord J. Allen

www.ingramcontent.com/pod-product-compliance
Lightning Source LLC
Chambersburg PA
CBHW060517290526
45791CB00001B/421